DEATH TO THE INQUISITIVE!
A Story Of Sinful Love

by

Lurana W. Sheldon

Double 9
BOOKS

Death To The Inquisitive!
A Story Of Sinful Love
by Lurana W. Sheldon

Copyright © 2023

All Rights reserved.

ISBN: 978-93-57487-26-9

Published by

DOUBLE 9 BOOKS

2/13-B, Ansari Road
Daryaganj, New Delhi – 110002
info@double9books.com
www.double9books.com
Tel. 011-40042856

ABOUT THE AUTHOR

Author of novels, poetry, short stories, and newspaper editor Lurana W. Sheldon (after marriage, Ferris; pen names, Richard Hackstaff, Stanley Norris, Grace Shirley). She was born in Hadlyme, Connecticut, on April 11, 1862. She said that she has worked in fifteen distinct and entirely diverse professions to support herself, including bookkeeping, journalism, employment in a chemical laboratory, purchasing grocery, and story writing. She advocated for women's suffrage and was anti-prohibition. Sheldon was the first poet in the US to contribute to the fight for birth control. Sheldon worked for over seven years at hospitals, including two years at the Woman's Medical College of the New York Infirmary, where he assisted doctors in a variety of ways. Sheldon visited the United States, Nova Scotia, and Newfoundland despite her unwell state. She married Judge Isaac F. Ferris of York County, Maine, who had previously worked as a journalist, on November 20, 1904 (or November 20, 1903). She passed away childless on June 11, 1945 in Maine.

CONTENTS

"Nay, do not ask—
In pity from the task forbear:
Smile on—nor venture to unmask
Man's heart, and view the Hell that's there."

CHAPTER I.
THE WHITECHAPEL MYSTERY.

Hark! It is a woman's cry
Echoing thro' the unhallowed place:—
Forward, to her rescue, fly—
See the suffering in her face.

A piercing shriek echoed throughout the entire length and breadth of the gloomy passage, hushed as it was in the brief hour of repose that usually intervened between the vice-rampant hour of midnight and the ever reluctant dawn.

It seemed as if the very light shrank from penetrating the loathsome windings of that wretched quarter of London, and as to pure air, it simply refused to enter such illy ventilated nooks and crevices, while the poisoned vapors that filled the narrow precincts were always trying to escape and failing through their own over-weight of reeking odors.

The scream of the dying woman was carried indistinctly to the ears of the sleeping inmates simply because the air was too heavy with vile tobacco and whiskey, stale beer fumes, and the exhalations of festering garbage heaps to transmit anything in other than a confused and indistinct manner.

Nevertheless there was something so extraordinarily frightful in the shriek that it did succeed in reaching the ears of nearly every habitue of the place, who, shrieking in their turn aroused the others, and one by one frowzeled heads and wrinkled faces issued from broken windows and rapidly, with shuffling footsteps, men and women crawled from innumerable dark passages and darker doorways, and with suspicious glances at each other, sneaked in and out through the slime and rubbish, in a half curious, half frightened search for a glimpse of that horrible tragedy.

I say *sneaked* about, and I use the word advisedly as the lawyers say, inasmuch as these degraded members of the human family,—these de-humanized fag ends of the genius Homo, did not walk, run, or perform any other specified motion in their perambulations.

On the contrary, they hugged the walls and the gutters; they were distrustful of the laws of gravitation and equilibrium, preferring to lean more or less heavily on walls and other supports, with bodies bent and faces averted, while the rapidity with which they appeared and disappeared was best appreciated by the Police who were supposed to guard this particular section of Whitechapel, but who religiously confined their guardianship to the outer walls, while the denizens of the multitudinous alleys or passages were free to perpetrate their murders, ply their nefarious trades and revel and rot in the stench of their own degradations.

One by one these creatures crawled from their hiding places.

Men were seen clutching the rags of their scanty clothing while their bleared eyes scanned every inch of the broken pavements.

Women, with odd garments thrown carelessly about their shoulders, joined in the search, and for a brief time no word was spoken.

Finally an old creature, dirtier if possible than the rest, bent in form, and with one long brown fang extending down over her shrunken chin, hobbled from a gloomy doorway and in a strident, nasal tone gave her opinion to these searchers of iniquity.

"Hit's Queen Liz thet's done fer, HI knowed 'er yell; You'll find 'er somewheres down by the Chinaman's shanty. HI spects 'e's knifed 'er."

"Good enough for 'er, the stuck hup 'uzzy," exclaimed one of the wretched beings that followed closely at the woman's heels.

"To think of 'er livin' 'ere for two years hand not speakin' to no one but that greasy yaller-skin. HI knowed 'e'd get sick of 'er 'fore long."

"S'pose you think hit's your turn next," snapped up another bedraggled female, whereupon a vicious battle ensued between the two while the men and women halted in their search to watch, what to them was the very essence of life, —a fight.

But the old crone who had first spoken crawled on until she reached the Chinaman's quarters, and there sure enough, a Mongolian, swarthy and greasy, his beady eyes blazing with excitement, was bending over and trying with poor success to withdraw a villainous looking weapon, half knife, half dagger, from the breast of an apparently dying woman.

The victim was a familiar figure in the Alley, and her clean, handsome face with its "hands-off" expression had long since won her the name of "Queen Liz."

While her failure to mingle with the other women or receive the beastly attentions of the men had made her an object of hatred to all concerned, still she had won their respect by her evident ability to defend herself at all times and in all circumstances, while the love she plainly bore her beautiful babe, a child of about two years, was a never ceasing source of wonderment and ridicule to these hardened mortals.

It was true that Queen Liz spent much time in the quarters of this particular Mongolian while there were many more eligible parties of her own nationality in the passage, but Queen Liz was evidently above her station, and as the Mongolian in question was possessed of more worldly goods than were his neighbors, it was reasonably supposed that she sought the comforts and luxuries of Chinese fans and Oolong in preference to the other shanties with their ever prevalent aroma of stale beer.

Nevertheless Queen Liz was not wholly overwhelmed by the wealth of Sam Hop Lee, because it was rumored that at certain intervals a gentleman from the outside world; a member of actual London society was seen going in and out of the narrow passage, Liz always accompanying him on these exits and entrances, for protection, it was generally supposed.

The sight of the stranger in their own lawful precincts brought always a mixture of sentiments to the thieves and sharpers who infested these gloomy byways.

Here was an excellent opportunity for operations in their own particular line of business, but here also was a woman armed with the usual weapons of the alley, ready and anxious to meet in mortal combat any and all that should dare lay hands upon herself or guest.

Thus Queen Liz was let pretty severely alone by all, and her life past and present was a mystery too obscure to be in any danger of being solved by the beer muddled brains of her neighbors.

But now Queen Liz was lying in the slime and mud of the alley with the deadly knife sticking firmly in her side, and as this uncanny assemblage of human scavengers drew nearer, Sam Lee gave one more vigorous pull at the weapon, and withdrawing it, turned its blade to the light of a flickering tallow dip, and instantly, in the eyes of each and every one present, he was acquitted of the horrible deed.

The knife was of a make unknown in the alley and only to be found in the possession of a man to whom money is no object and who could well afford to follow his own fancies in the design of his favorite paper cutter, for such the weapon evidently was.

Long, narrow and sharply pointed, the blade was of finest silver, handsomely engraved, and the ebony handle shone resplendent with gems, so placed as to form on the polished surface the initials M. S. in dazzling characters.

CHAPTER II.
A SUICIDAL ATTEMPT.

Have pity, Reader,'twas the fire
Of human passion in her brain,—
First, youth's impulsive, mad desire,
Then love, and love's devouring pain.

Some two years previous to the incidents of our opening chapter, in a quiet house situated on G—St., in the vicinity of Belmont Square, an aged couple sat quietly talking, while the shadows fell longer and darker about the room, and the increased tread of passing feet spoke plainly of the end of another day of that weary labor that fell to the lot of the large number of tradespeople who lived in this row of modest houses.

The aged couple mentioned were occupying the two narrow windows that faced the crowded thoroughfare, and the two faces were pressed anxiously against the glass, while the old eyes peered eagerly up and down, over and across in a careful search for the one of whom they had been quietly speaking.

There was silence for a little while and then the old man leaned back in his chair and, while wiping the moisture from his glasses with a generous square of cambric, said querulously:

"It is mighty strange, Marthy, where Lizzie is. She ought to be home before this."

"I know it, father," responded his wife meekly. "She's been acting very strange of late, staying away from home and coming in at all hours as dragged out as if she had been walking the streets for miles."

"Maybe that's what she does," snapped the old man, and then, as if ashamed of his hasty words, he added in a softer tone: "Though why she should do that I can't see. She's got a good home here with us and has had ever since our poor Mary died and left us our grandchild in the place of our child to care for and protect."

"And we've done both, father," said the old lady, gently. "Lizzie has no need to seek pleasure outside her own home, what, with the rooms to look after, her books, her piano and her needle work, she ought to be pretty well contented."

"That's so, Marthy, but she evidently is not. Now ever since that young man rented our two back rooms and began to spend his evenings here—"

"You don't think she is in love with him, do you father?" interrupted his wife quickly.

"Can't say, Marthy, you women can judge better of that. I only know she acts uncommonly unhappy lately. Let's see, the young fellow has been gone a week now, hasn't he?"

"Yes, that is so, and Lizzie has seemed all broke down ever since. I was asking her yesterday to see Mr. Jeller, but she turned as white as anything.

"'No, no, Grandma,' she said, 'I'll not see any doctors. There's nothing the matter with me, nothing!'

"But there was a hard look came into her eyes, and the idea went through my mind that perhaps that gentlemanly looking fellow was just playing with her after all, and she had only found it out after her heart was gone from her."

Here the old lady stopped to wipe the tears from her faded eyes, while the blood of his youth flushed her husband's face and, with cane uplifted, he muttered fiercely:

"If I thought that, I'd cane him, old as I am! Lizzie's a good girl and has been as well raised and as well educated as the best of them, and if her father and grandfather before him were tradespeople, they were honest and respectable, and I don't know what better dowry a woman can need than her own virtues and accomplishments and a record behind her of generations of honorable people."

Here the old man again sank back in his chair, overcome by the violence of his emotions, while his wife, re-adjusting her glasses, moved aside the curtain and again peered out into the fast darkening street.

There was silence for a few moments and then her husband resumed his position at the other window, while the ticking of the clock echoed, painfully distinct, through the silent room, and the sound of passing feet grew fainter and fainter, and darkness, mingling with the impenetrable vapors of a London fog, settled heavily down upon the earth.

Certainly no girl could have a more happy home or two more tender, loving companions than had Elizabeth Merril.

But discontent is bred in the bone and needs no outward influence or surroundings to foster its soul destroying germs.

Elizabeth had grown into womanhood, beautiful in form and feature, loyal in heart and spotless in her maidenly purity, but the seeds of discontent, inherited or otherwise, sprang up in her heart and took from every pleasure that fullness of joy which is so necessary to perfect happiness.

It was her suggestion to rent the superfluous rooms thereby adding to the family exchequer and at the same time increasing her household duties.

The logic was excellent, but the impulse of a dissatisfied mind prompted the suggestion and evil impulses, however logical, are rarely productive of good results.

This particular instance was a most conclusive proof of the veracity of such reasoning.

For a few brief weeks Elizabeth's heart was filled with content and peace. With her additional labor came renewed ambition and the results seemed highly satisfactory to all concerned.

Then, as time passed on and the young man who occupied the rooms found many and varied excuses for seeking her presence, the roses on Elizabeth's cheeks deepened into carnation, her eyes flashed with a new born glory, and from morn till night the tender song of the nightingale burst joyously from her lips.

The young man had occupied the rooms for nearly a year and his devotion to their grandchild had been constantly growing more marked.

But for the past few months the song had ceased on Elizabeth's lips and the rosy cheeks were growing steadily paler.

In vain the aged couple watched and questioned, but Elizabeth's feminine tact and spirit outwitted them.

She fulfilled her duties patiently, as of yore, but would seize upon every possible pretext for remaining away from home, and now, during the week that her lover failed to appear at his cosy apartments, they had hardly seen her for more than a few moments each day.

Thus it was no wonder that to-night they watched and waited at their narrow windows while the hours stole by and still the wandering girl returned not to her pleasant home.

Back and forth over the great London Bridge she was walking; her head bent low; her blue eyes fixed and glaring; her pale lips compressed in bitter agony, while over and over again she paused and looked eagerly down into the sluggish water.

The bridge was jammed as usual with hurrying pedestrians and jostling carts, and few turned to look at the solitary figure.

Now and then a watchful "Bobby" stopped and stared into her face and more than one of these experienced officers read the signs of coming trouble in her pallid features.

But it was not their duty to ask her business or order her away. She was doing no harm and surely it would be but a meddlesome act on their part to try and avert the danger which they so plainly foresaw.

Still she walked on and on until the crowd was lessened and fewer officers remained on duty.

Just as the fog, rising from the river below and the smoke falling from the chimneys above, met and mingled in a pall of gloom and obscurity, she turned again, paused, looked once more into the darkness below, then vaulting suddenly to the massive rail, sprang lightly forward through the mists and down into the awful waters.

CHAPTER III.
RESCUED BY THIEVES.

And these are men,—these creatures bold,
Who live to plunder and to kill;
Formed in the Great Creator's mold
But subject to the Devil's will.

If all committers of this deed of questionable cowardice would choose so opportune a moment for their rashness as did Elizabeth, they would probably live to see the error of their ways and to realize that the things we know are better than the things we know not of, but it is rarely that one so determined as she to terminate a wretched existence is thwarted in that desire by the presence of rescuers, but such was the case in this instance.

Two men of the type commonly known in London as wharf "rats" or dock and river thieves, were slowly sculling along under cover of the intense fog on the lookout for plunder of any and every sort.

Naturally, when Elizabeth's body struck the water not ten feet from their craft, they stopped sculling and quickly investigated the nature of the prey that had so literally fallen into their hands.

Elizabeth was pulled into the boat apparently lifeless, and in less time than it takes to chronicle the event, was shorn of her pretty rings, purse and outer garments.

A folded paper pinned securely to the lining of her waist was also promptly removed by the thief and thrust carelessly into the outer pocket of his coat as he doubtless thought it of little consequence, and only confiscated it through a natural impulse of greed and robbery.

Then the younger of the two proceeded to fasten a heavy lead around her waist, and lifting her carefully in his arms was about to lower the body once more into the silent river whose waters had already swallowed up and forever concealed innumerable secrets of like nature, when a flash from his partner's lantern falling upon Elizabeth's upturned face revealed to him her exceeding loveliness and awoke within him an instinct, whether brutal or humane, we shall shortly determine.

"Oh, Oiy soiy, Bill, this 'ere lass is too bloomin' 'ansome tew feed de fishes wid," he said, "and she ben't derd, nurther," he added, as he noticed Elizabeth's breath returning in short, faint gasps. "Ben't hoften we picks hup such fine goods as dese," he continued, while a fiendish expression passed over his swarthy face. "Blowed if Oiy doesn't think Oiy'll confiscate dis fer m' hown use," and he drew Elizabeth's still senseless form across his knee.

"Put'er down, Jemmy! Cawn't you wait till you gets to de dock or does yer want ter stay hout 'n dis 'ere fog hall night?" said the older man gruffly, adding authoritatively: "Cover de gal hup in de bottom, she'll keep! Oiy'm wet tew de' ide. Come, scull along hor we wont get 'ome till midnight."

Whether it was the fragments of original humanity that made him refuse to witness the desecration of helplessness, or whether he possessed sufficient of the brute instinct to enjoy with keener relish the struggles of a frenzied woman in the hands of an unprincipled and determined villain, we can not tell;—

At any rate Elizabeth was allowed to lie quietly under an old sail in the bottom of the boat, returning slowly, but with such perfect control to acute consciousness that she allowed no sound of either fear or suffering to escape her lips.

She overheard enough of their conversation, during the row down the river to show her who her rescuers were and what her ultimate fate would be unless she could escape from their clutches. She realized that even her unfortunate condition would give her no mercy in their hands and might rather be a source of more intense gratification to their fiendish and inhuman desires. Reason told her to remain perfectly passive, as it was evident they only awaited her return to consciousness for the furtherance of their diabolical plans.

Even when the boat bumped heavily against the wharf, turned back and veered about in a most extraordinary manner and the damp fog of the river was exchanged for the foul stench of sewer gas and garbage floats, and she realized, with a feeling of horror, that they were gliding, not by, but under the dock, still she made no sound.

At last they stopped by a rotten ladder; the boat was tied and the younger man sprang hastily up the slippery steps and thrust open, with his shoulder, a heavy trap door.

Then the older of the two raised Elizabeth from the boat and passed her up through the narrow opening to the man above. He then followed and after a hasty consultation between the two she was left, as the young "rat" expressed it, "soif fer de present," on a pile of rags in the corner of the cellar.

Then, apparently regardless whether she lived or died, they ascended another rickety ladder and the sullen gleam of their lantern was soon lost to sight in the darkness above.

Elizabeth waited until the sound of their footsteps had passed away, then rising hastily, she began groping about in the darkness for the ladder which she had so dimly discerned by the light of the smoking lantern.

Now every thing was dark, and the knowledge of that yawning trap-door and perhaps more just like it under her very feet, made her almost insane with fear. All desire for a watery death had vanished from her mind. Her lungs were so filled with nauseous gases that it was with a feeling of almost frantic joy she touched the rungs of the worm-eaten ladder and prepared to climb to the landing above.

The upper Hall was narrow, dirty and perfectly dark. Elizabeth groped her way carefully along, holding firmly to the wall, but could see no outlet or glimmer of light either before her or above, but knowing that to turn back would be but rushing to a fate far worse than death, she pressed eagerly forward, peering into the impenetrable darkness, while occasionally a great, slimy rat scampered across her foot, or a loathsome bat, with a sudden rush, passed so near her face that she turned sick with horror and held to the heavy walls with all her strength.

CHAPTER IV.
THE SHAME-BORN CHILD.

Calm Death,—Thou comest not to such as these,—
Their griefs affright thee,—their sad faces fail to please.

Probably the length of time that elapsed (which seemed like an eternity to Elizabeth,) was, in reality, not more than half an hour before a ray of light greeted her eyes, coming through a ragged chink in the crumbling masonry of the heavy walls.

Creeping cautiously forward she put her eye to the crevice and looked eagerly into the inner room.

The scene she witnessed was well calculated to chill the blood of an able bodied man, but to a delicate woman, still trembling from the effects of her awful plunge into the river;—hampered by dripping garments and nearly frantic with the fear of momentary violence, the sight was more than doubly horrible.

The room was nothing more than a large vault or closet built into the solid walls, probably for no definite purpose, but so well adapted to its present use that one would think its designer must have foreseen its ultimate fate.

Several battered and smoking lanterns hung on nails, which had been wedged firmly between loose bricks in the decaying walls, their outlines appearing to her excited imagination not unlike the red eye balls and smoke begrimed faces of the score of beings upon whom their dismal glimmer fell.

This score of individuals, representing a class of monsters, born in the slime of cellars; nourished on the odors of decomposition and trained to accomplishments of vice and evil, were busy at the ghoulish work of robbing two human bodies, whose swollen and livid members plainly proclaimed them trophies from the river's unfailing supply.

Ragged females with bloated faces and keen eyes were squabbling like cats over the articles which had been removed from the dead woman's body, while the males cursed and struck at each other in a frantic struggle for the watch and jewels which the other water-soaked victim had worn.

The scene was horrible, pile upon pile of rubbish was heaped about the room, and one and all seemed interested in claiming and getting possession of as much plunder as they could, by fair means or foul.

Elizabeth plainly identified her rescuers who were among the most quarrelsome of the lot, but, even in her bewilderment, she noticed that there was no mention made of *their* evenings work or of her body, which, of course, they supposed was safe in the recesses of that loathsome cellar.

At this instant a vague thought flitted through her mind as to what booty her body had afforded them. She felt for her rings, but they were gone. She thrust her hand into the bosom of her dress for her watch, and her lips grew white as ashes, while a new horror, passing through her brain, overcame for the moment all fear of personal violence. The paper which had been safe in her bosom when she sprang from the bridge was not there. She had determined that the secret which it held should die with her, but now that her plan for death had failed, the recovery of that treasured paper must be the whole aim and purpose of her life.

Again the miserable creature who had rescued her from death became the unknowing instrument of her good fortune.

The young thief, whom she recognized as "Bill," became violently angry over the unequal distribution of the jewels and, throwing off his coat, struck wildly at his partner, while the others proceeded with their individual bickerings, apparently unconscious of the pugilistic encounter.

The coat in falling obscured, in a measure, Elizabeth's view of the inner room.

She had lost all thought of fear in her wild determination to secure the missing paper.

Pushing her hand cautiously into the hole in the masonry she dislodged a portion of brick with little trouble, then forcing her white arm carefully through the opening she touched the coat and pulled it gently aside.

Her idea was simply to gain another unobstructed view of the room, but accidently her fingers touched the edge of a folded paper protruding from the pocket, and quick as flash Elizabeth closed her fingers upon it and drew it toward her through the hole. She could not see it, but the familiarity of touch and feeling convinced her that it was her bosom companion for the past ten months, and even in the excitement and danger of the situation she stood motionless for a moment while she pressed it fervently to her lips.

Then, taking advantage of a particularly noisy scuffle, Elizabeth slipped softly by the door. The terrors of nightmare were upon her. She imagined she heard them pursuing her but could not run for fear of falling in the darkness; pitching down some hidden trap or making some accidental sound that would tell them of her presence.

At last, after almost innumerable windings, a glimmer of electric light came down upon her through a cellar grating which opened directly upon the street. A little further on and another flight of worm eaten steps were before her. Up these she climbed, and raised, with all her strength a heavy grating, then, feeling once more the pure air upon her brow and the sense of freedom in her soul, she reeled and fell heavily forward, like an inanimate body, upon the damp, gray curb stone. How long she lay there she could not tell, but the bell of a distant cathedral, tolling the hour of midnight, aroused her, and she crawled along until her strength in a measure returned, then, rising, she walked as quickly as possible away from this terrible neighborhood. On and on she went, her strength failing her at every step, until once more exhausted she sank down before the gateway of a large building, which, fortunately for her, proved to be a Hospital.

Here she was found by a resident physician on his return from the Opera in the early morning hours.

Some time during the following day an employee of the Hospital discovered a soiled and water-stained Marriage Certificate, which the wind had evidently blown behind the massive gates. The Certificate was placed in the physician's private desk for safe keeping, but no connection between it and the suffering woman was ever suspected.

Elizabeth was placed immediately in the ward, and every care given her, but for four weeks she hovered between life and death, raving of murder, robbery, suicide and all such frightful happenings, until the anxious physician feared for her reason as well as for her life. It was not until her child was born, a month after her entrance, that she gained, either mentally or physically, but after another four weeks of excellent nursing she was discharged from the Hospital as needing no further treatment.

She had given the authorities a false name in an almost involuntary effort toward self-protection and the concealment of her degradation, receiving at their hands that disinterested and strictly impartial attention bestowed upon all their patients. She was to them but one of thousands who drift on the shoals of sin and are left to perish, or are floated off by the tide of life to a longer struggle and a fiercer death on the ragged rocks of crime, therefore it was only natural that her case elicited no special comment from the busy officials. Thus, sick at heart, homeless, friendless, with no money, and with her shame-born child resting heavily upon her arm, Elizabeth went forth once more into the streets of London.

CHAPTER V.
MAURICE SINCLAIR.

The storm that tears the human heart
With deepest furrows, leaves its trace
Like shadows from a passing cloud
Upon the mirror of the face.

Passing through Portland Place, at about the hour of eleven, on that damp, foggy night, it would have been impossible not to notice the most attractive of the many beautiful houses, for there emanated from its windows such a blaze of light that even the dense vapor that obscured all objects in its near vicinity was penetrated by the brilliancy for some distance.

The carriages that stopped before its portals loomed up through the mist like phantoms, while the guests that entered the spacious door only lost their ghastliness as they emerged into the full glare of the inner hall during the brief moment of transit.

It was very evident that a ball of more than ordinary magnificence was in progress, and one glance at the face of the hostess, Mrs. Archibald Sinclair, would have shown any intelligent observer that, to Mrs. Sinclair, at least, the necessity for making this particular entertainment a glorious success was so urgent that it destroyed, in a measure, her own enjoyment. Yet, with the innate tact of a woman born to receive, to entertain, and to genuinely please her guests, all trace of anxiety was carefully concealed, all nervousness overcome, and only affability and satisfaction were allowed reflection upon her expressive countenance.

However, in spite of her complacent demeanor, there were few mothers present at that reception but could readily appreciate her feelings and who did not, in their inmost hearts, admire her diplomatic tact during so trying an ordeal.

Not a few carefully modulated voices signified to each other their opinion and approval of her manner, for the gossips were out in full force that evening. They knew by long anticipation that food for their insatiable appetites would be furnished on this occasion in the person, manner and language of Maurice

Sinclair, their hostess' enigmatical son, who had so lately returned from the Great Desert of Gobi or some other equally undesirable quarter of the earth's surface.

True, rumor had it that this eccentric young man had been seen in and about the City at intervals during the past year, but as any allusion made to the widow, his mother, on this subject, met with unapproachable silence, the matter was prudently dropped, and the information derived from newspapers and casual observers accepted or rejected according to the minds of the hearers, in the absence of better authority.

Many of the matrons present this evening recalled, only too accurately, the days when Maurice Sinclair's boyish pranks refused for him admission to one school after another. His wrong doings were always of a nature too delicate for public mention and, after a more than usually disgraceful affair while he was only fifteen years of age, he suddenly vanished, and, but a month later, Archibald Sinclair, his disappointed father, was laid to rest in the family plot, leaving behind a sorrowing wife and a nearly heart-broken mother.

At last, after five years had elapsed, Mrs. Sinclair, tired of the great house, and the wealth and splendor which she could never enjoy in solitude, adopted a distant relative, a beautiful girl of sixteen, and upon her she lavished the love of her true womanly heart and the wealth that flowed so abundantly into her coffers from many sources.

Stella Ives, or Stella Sinclair as she was afterwards called, was one of those peculiarly beautiful women, combining that which is most rarely seen, beauty of face and form, with great depth of character and unusual mental precocity. Now, at the age of twenty-one, Stella stood peerless among her companions. Her wavy yellow hair fell low over a broad white forehead. Her hazel eyes shone with the clear light of a brilliant intellect. Her mouth was large, but shapely and sweet, and, in laughing, disclosed a set of faultless teeth that were at once the envy and admiration of all. Stella was a little above medium height, plump and graceful, and withal a girl whom all could admire, but whose natural reserve held aloof from her shrine the many lovers who would gladly pay their homage to so fair a divinity.

Ten years had passed since Maurice disappeared and now, like one risen from the dead, he had returned and, in a brief but affectionate note, stated his intention to assist in entertaining her guests on this particular evening. He explained his non-appearance since reaching London as due to sensitiveness about meeting the mother whom he had so deeply grieved, but having heard of his adopted sister's "coming out" reception, he could control himself no longer and would throw himself humbly and unreservedly upon her mercy.

Only an hour before the time for her guests to arrive Mrs. Sinclair called Stella to her luxurious dressing-room and, passing her arm around the young girl's form, said fondly: "Stella dear, look your best to-night. You know we expect a large contingent of lords and baronets, and nothing fills my old heart with more exquisite pleasure than to witness the admiration which they bestow upon my beautiful daughter."

Stella laughed softly, but no blush of foolish vanity rose in her face at her foster-mother's tender words. She only pressed the matronly arm affectionately and replied, "All right, mamma, I will do my best. But you are sure it is because of the 'lords and baronets' that you wish me to look my best? Confess now," she continued archly, "is it not because you wish the first glimpse of his adopted sister to be a satisfactory one to Maurice that you take this violent interest?"

A little disconcerted by the young girl's reading of her secret, Mrs. Sinclair could only laugh and push her gently from the room.

After Stella had gone, Mrs. Sinclair sank down on the sofa by the heavily draped window to hold brief communion with herself as was her wont when questions or thoughts of more than usual importance arose in her mind. There was only a few moments in which to thus commune, but Mrs. Sinclair possessed that distinctly feminine ability to evolve various extraordinary theories on a given subject and yet deduct therefrom a logical conclusion in about half the time it would take a less intuitive brain to lose itself completely in an inextricable tangle of reasons and vagaries. "The past is past," was her conclusion.

"My son will to-night be under my roof; I must begin at the beginning; there shall be no reproaches. I shall offer him love, money, home, influence and a fair chance of winning a beautiful wife. If he refuses these, there is nothing more."

So saying, she rose, and with a hopeful look in her eyes, passed, in her own stately and gracious manner, down the wide staircase and on into the spacious parlors of her beautiful home, now doubly attractive to her by the anticipated happiness of her son's return.

For, although there was little doubt but that the erratic Maurice had been in London for many months, yet he had not seen fit to gladden his mother's heart with the sight of his almost forgotten face until just in time to give Stella's birthday reception a double significance.

CHAPTER VI.
A PAINFUL REMINISCENCE.

How few look back upon a past
Of spotless purity,—and who
Would dare absolve with prayer and fast
The deeds they've done—the deeds they do;

Whatever may be the prejudice existing against the customary shams, deceptions and hypocrisies of society, certainly the sugar coating which good breeding and etiquette throw over the many bitter and disagreeable ingredients that go to make up our daily lives, is very palatable and pleasing. Suspicions may be aroused; curiosity be on the *qui vive*, anxiety and interest waging violent warfare in the human heart, yet the restrictions and obligations of courtesy demand self-control and affable manners, while gentle words make smooth many sharp and jagged corners in life's mental conflict, that uncovered would oftentimes cause friction and discomfort.

In vain the gossips looked and listened for some fragment of food for their customary *menu*, but neither Mrs. Sinclair or Stella showed by look or word that this particular reception was fraught with more than the usual interest, and as to the long lost son, his sojourn among the heathen nations of the earth, seemed to both foster and expand his naturally courteous disposition. His meeting with his mother had been cordial in the extreme. There was no time for lavish demonstration of affection, as he only arrived a brief ten minutes before the earliest guest. His presentation to his adopted sister, however, was marked by a change of demeanor that was plainly observed by all, yet, no person present, so far overcame the feeling of wonder that his manner generated, as to even boast of an approximate guess regarding its cause. The look that came into his wide, gray eyes when they first fell upon the beautiful girl, was one of amazement, and the gossips instantly concluded that beautiful women had been rare in his experience. Then a lurid light gleamed in his eyeballs; the lines of his face became drawn and tense, and hatred, and envy, were instantly ascribed to him. But as he touched her hand in greeting, a look so plainly indicative of carnal passion gleamed in every feature of his now diabolical face, that cold shivers and sensations of horror, swept through the sympathetic natures present, and doubtless, the maids and matrons, would have risen *en-masse* and called for their carriages, had not the sudden withdrawal of Stella's hand, brought back, as if by magic, the winning smile to the young man's countenance and transformed him again, in an instant, into the hero of the evening.

The dowagers reasoned that their lorgnettes were dimmed and their visions contorted thereby, while the maidens, serene in their innocence, forgot in a brief time the glimpse they had, or fancied they had, into man's inmost nature, and vied with each other in their efforts to win the approval of so distinguished and withal so mysterious a parti. Possibly a vague thought of this young scion's probable inheritance brought favorable influence to bear upon the stricter morals of the scheming mammas, as social position and wealth have heretofore and probably always will weigh successfully in the balance against questionable character and immorality.

Nevertheless, so strong was the momentary resemblance between this fascinating young man and the numerous likenesses of the mythical Beelzebub, that the Lady Van Tyne assured her family physician, in a strictly confidential interview the next morning, that, "for an instant it seemed as if the very curls of auburn hair stood up on his temples like horns, and she was sure that almost countless numbers of hooked and venomous claws protruded from his dainty patent leather boots, while as to his face,"—here she shuddered with a convulsive, reminiscent spasm, "it was the face of Satan himself!"

The good Doctor listened and sympathized; prescribed a pleasing tonic and rendered a modest bill, but he was afterward heard to say to his assistant, quite unprofessionally, of course. "It's wonderful what champagne will do. If the ladies would only stick to Bass, now!"

The Lady Van Tyne and her family physician were on the very best of terms, however.

It had been remarked by many that Dr. Seward was the only human being whom the wilful lady feared or felt disposed in any particular to obey.

But both the physician and his proud patron still bore in undying remembrance a little episode of early days, and for reasons of mutual interest, their friendship remained firm and unimpeachable.

Thirty years before, Lady Van Tyne was a plump, pretty brunette of eighteen, or rather, such was the charming Isabel Montfort, for the wealthy Sir Casper Van Tyne had not as yet secured her for his bride, and Dr. Seward was but a beginner in the fascinating science which later brought him fame and fortune.

Now, whenever he saw the Lady Van Tyne, his thoughts involuntarily wandered back to the summer day when, with consternation in her face, Lady Montfort had called upon him with the vivacious Isabel to secure his immediate and most careful services.

The good lady readily accepted his verdict and in all innocence prepared her daughter for the immediate journey to America, which the imperative physician prescribed.

Little did the good woman realize that all her elaborate preparations were smiled at, more or less sadly, by her daughter and the clever physician.

For, instead of the extended trip across the ocean, Miss Isabel betook herself quietly to the private residence of the physician, and there for three months she remained under the careful surveillance of doctor and nurse.

The ruse was more than successful, inasmuch as Miss Isabel was restored to her mother, and Sir Casper's eager arms, in rapidly improving health, while the young physician's somewhat astounding fee was quietly paid by a gentleman of excellent social standing who was, moreover, the husband of one of the most charming and estimable ladies of Dr. Seward's acquaintance.

The secret had been well guarded. Now and then a dull pang of self-reproach was experienced by the physician when he remembered how indifferent he had been to the fate of the child after he had secured a home and guardianship for it. He watched it more or less interestedly for about ten years, as he also watched that other boy so singularly alike in feature but so widely different in parentage and social prospects.

The boys, at ten and eleven respectively, were as near alike as brothers, but from that time on there were changes in the adopted parents mode of life, and the child of unsanctified love vanished from his gaze forever.

Into the lives of all physicians there come many and varied episodes of private nature, but probably of all the secret games indulged in by unscrupulous human beings, that one is best remembered wherein they hold so prominent a hand.

It was little wonder, in the light of such reflections, that Dr. Seward evinced not only a slight irritability regarding his patient's hallucination, but also a most extraordinary desire to see this young man whose personal appearance was so suggestive of the Infernal Regions.

CHAPTER VII.
THE BREATH OF PASSION.

The torch-light of Passion, how fierce is its power—
It wakens, it burns, it consumes in an hour;
Accursed is the mortal who feels its hot breath,
For the end is destruction—destruction and death.

Unfortunately for the fate of her future, Stella did not see the extraordinary expression on the young man's face that caused such mental consternation among her guests.

The thrill which vibrated through her entire being at the touch of his firm hand rendered her incapable for the moment of meeting his eyes.

So strong was the current of magnetism that passed between them that the mingled sensations of fear and bewilderment forced her to withdraw her hand with so much vehemence that she was obliged, from an innate sense of courtesy, to make a trifling remark to cover the seeming rudeness of her action.

So swift was the transformation in his face, that, when her eyes were finally raised to his, only the sweetest of smiles wreathed his proud, passionate lips, and the glance he bent upon her, was one of mingled reverence and admiration.

In vain the dowagers angled and the maidens blushed and simpered.

Maurice Sinclair moved about among the guests, always charming and attentive, but his expressive eyes followed Stella in her every motion and seemed to devour her beauty with an intensity so deep as to render him unconscious even to his own enchantment.

Only one of the gentlemen present had noticed particularly the greeting between Maurice and Stella, or if they had, man-like, they had attached no significance to the expression whatsoever, and would undoubtedly have reasoned, had their opinions been asked on the subject, that a man's face often expresses sentiments foreign to his nature, and that a fellow could hardly be called to account for the idiosyncrasies and caprices of unruly features.

But Sir Frederic Atherton had, for reasons of his own, been a keen observer of Maurice's face, and a look of loathing crossed his own noble countenance as he muttered, almost audibly, a word that sounded singularly like "cur." But as he noted the magical effect on Stella, he drew a long sigh which was as promptly checked with a firm closing of the lips, and stepping quickly forward actually stood between the two, then offering his arm to Stella with a laughing remark, he led her away, from a glance, which in his honorable soul, seemed like desecration.

Sir Frederic was nearly forty years of age; a man marvelously blessed by nature, in that he possessed not only a magnificent bearing; a face grand in its determination and strength; but a mental calibre as well, unequaled by another of his associates. To these he had added integrity and justice; winning the confidence of all by his honorable dealings both in social and business relations.

Women worshiped and followed him; Yea, they even flung themselves at his very feet, but thus far in life Sir Frederic had remained "heart whole and fancy free," while the memory of a good mother and a faithful sister saved him from being, like the majority of men whom women flatter, a chronic disbeliever in the chastity of their sex. Always courteous and gentle, it was no wonder that women and children loved and trusted him. Strong and honorable, it was only natural for men to give him confidence and respect, and he whom his fellow-men regard is sure to be of all men the most trustworthy.

The love of woman may be but the consequence of perfect features, manly proportions or a musical voice, but the regard of man for man comes only as the result of sterling worth.

For some time Sir Frederic had been questioning himself regarding the quality of his affection for Mrs. Sinclair's beautiful adopted daughter, but not until he saw her, a delicate flower, exposed if only for a second to the baneful light of an evil eye, did he realize how deeply and dearly he loved Stella. The truth stabbed him like a knife, but after the first sharp pain, and as he felt her hand upon his arm, a joy surged through his being that the forty well spent years of his life had hitherto failed to bring him.

After a moment's conversation with Mrs. Sinclair, Stella was again led away by one of Her Majesty's officers for a sprightly polka, and Sir Frederic glad to commune for a moment with his somewhat excited heart, moved a heavy chair farther into the shadow and sat down, while *his* eyes also watched the graceful movements of Stella, but with very different emotions from those which were rushing through Maurice Sinclair's brain at the same time.

Stella had danced with one after another of her guests and was seated for a moment's rest on a wide turkish divan in a shaded corner of the room.

It was only a moment, but Maurice's restless glance sought her out, and smiling his excuses into the baby face of Lady Isabel Van Tyne's youngest daughter, he, much to her disappointment, strolled across the room and stood before Stella with the subdued light of a chandelier brightening his wavy hair into glittering rings about his well shaped head.

"May I call you Stella?" he whispered abruptly, as he bent slightly toward her and rested one shapely white hand on a pot of rare exotics that helped to shade the sofa on which she rested.

Mrs. Sinclair was passing at that moment and the ring on Maurice's finger caught her eye. With a tender smile she laid her hand upon his and whispered softly, "How well I remember that ring, Maurice."

It was puzzling to Stella that he should appear so confused at this simple remark of his mother and withdraw his hand so rudely from her gentle clasp, but Mrs. Sinclair had passed quietly on, and remembering that his question remained unanswered she controlled her thoughts and responded frankly, "Certainly, Maurice, I should feel awkward enough to call you Mr. Sinclair after hearing and speaking the name of Maurice so frequently for so many years. I think, really, I almost consider you my own brother," she continued shyly, although a passing blush and an almost imperceptible hesitancy in her speech gave the pretty avowal an appearance of untruthfulness.

To the many eager observers of this momentary by-play, the avowal, judged by the eye alone, seemed almost a confession of a dearer sentiment than the sisterly affection to which she had so frankly laid claim.

Notwithstanding her words of Platonic friendship Maurice smiled as if well pleased, not only with the words but their silent contradiction. He sank gracefully upon the divan by her side and in so doing his hand accidently touched hers and in an instant there came again that expression of consuming passion that had darkened his face at their first meeting. Again the mesmeric spell of his presence was upon her. A sensation, this time wholly indescribable, passed over her frame and as before she was powerless to raise her eyes until the cloud was lifted and once more the calm of a summer sky was mirrored on his exquisite face.

Just at that instant a slight crash was heard near by and both started involuntarily from their momentary forgetfulness to ascertain the cause.

CHAPTER VIII.
A MIDNIGHT CRIME.

How oft men use the gifts of God
To aid their plans and cloak their sins;
At nightfall, silence reigns above
And deviltry on earth begins.

The noise was merely the shivering to atoms of a small venetian vase which stood on a diminutive ebony table not far from the divan on which Stella was seated.

Mrs. Sinclair had accidently struck the table, and the gossips declared afterward, in the privacy of their own Boudoirs, that she was watching her son at the very time when his accidental touching of Stella's hand had wrought so fearful a change upon his features, and, quite naturally, they argued that an intuitive fear for her adopted daughter's future made her hand unsteady. At any rate, she had turned suddenly pale and grasped the slender table for support with the result already mentioned.

Maurice sprang promptly forward, and motioning to a servant to remove the fragments of glass, offered his arm gracefully to his mother and passed up the room to where the Countess Martinet was sitting with her angular daughter.

Stella took this opportunity to join the Misses Huntington on a neighboring sofa and again the strains of music floated through the spacious parlors and partners were soon whirling gaily about in the witcheries of a glorious waltz.

Never had Stella looked so superbly beautiful as to-night, with the graceful folds of her exquisite white satin draperies clinging about her charming figure. The gold of her hair scintillated in myriad iridescent rays about her broad forehead and snowy neck, while the gleaming diamond star that shown upon her bosom vied with the sparkling lustre of her eye, and in the opinions of the gentlemen, at least, paled woefully in the comparison.

Before this enjoyable ball was over it was no wonder that hearts, adoration and homes were silently or in hurried, eager whispers, laid humbly upon the altar of love, and many an ardent lover went home that night to dream of heavenly raptures or exactly the reverse.

To Stella, however, the sentiment of all absorbing passion was, as yet unknown. Life was at its best and brightest with her, and the brief, inexplicable sensation of fear which she had felt at Maurice's touch, was the only cloud, small and visionary as it was, that in any way darkened the skies of her perfect happiness.

The fog was still resting heavily upon the earth when the last carriage rolled away and Maurice walked with his mother up the broad stairs to spend his first night in ten years beneath the parental roof.

Some way Stella lingered longer than usual that night over her adieux to Sir Frederic Atherton, but the fault, if fault it was, could not be laid at her door.

His carriage was the last and if he held her hand a moment longer than usual, she reasoned that, it was only because he had known her from childhood and now, at her debut into the world of womanly duties and pleasures, it was only natural that he should feel a desire to congratulate and perhaps advise her for her future welfare.

It was with this idea in mind that she let her hand rest quietly in his and raised her eyes so confidently to his face.

What she saw there was neither the courteous smile of congratulation or the benign bearing of one about to offer sage admonition. Instead, she saw a look of such ineffable tenderness bent upon her, that to her inmost soul there came an instantaneous sense of security, protection and sacred confidence, and tears suffused her lovely eyes in a blinding flood of gratitude which she was powerless to control.

Another instant and his lips had touched her golden hair, and the sound of the departing carriage told her he was gone.

With a curious feeling of loneliness and amazement thereat, she followed, almost in a dream, to Mrs. Sinclair's door.

Stella said good night as soon as possible, thinking that in all probability mother and son would wish to converse on many topics of interest, but as she passed from the room she turned and smiling sweetly, said, "I am sorry to usurp your old quarters in the west wing, Maurice, but we thought I had better not change as the south room might be more grateful to your warm country tastes."

With this slightly saucy allusion to his mysterious past, Stella kissed her finger tips to Mrs. Sinclair and closed the door softly behind her.

After Stella had gone Maurice seemed suddenly fatigued. The light vanished from his eyes and his tones grew languid, while a certain nervousness of manner betrayed to Mrs. Sinclair's acute perceptions the fact that, for some reason, her son felt ill at ease in his mother's presence.

Kissing him fondly she made haste to say, "Now darling, you had better go right to your room. We shall have plenty of time to talk in the future, for I am an old woman now and I trust my son will never feel like leaving me again."

"How old is Stella, mother?" was his somewhat irrelevant remark when she had finished speaking.

"She is twenty-one to day, my son, and I think you will agree that a sweeter, truer woman could hardly be imagined," responded his mother warmly.

"She is very beautiful," Maurice began, but checking himself, he said abruptly, "I have spent the last three years of my life wandering about in the heart of the Great Desert of Shamo, and some times I fancy the sulphurous fumes and heat of its burning lakes have impregnated my blood and tainted my whole system with a substance, which, although capable of overcoming other impurities, is but a poor choice between the natural and the acquired evil."

Here, seeing his mother's look of complete mystification, he paused and added playfully, "Ah, mother, I have frightened and perplexed you all ready: I must retire and to-morrow you shall say whether I am brute or human, for in truth, some times I can hardly tell." With these words he laughed a low, musical and extraordinarily joyous laugh that had attracted her once before that evening, then touching his mother's cheek lightly with his lips, went hurriedly from the room, through the hall and up the wide staircase.

On reaching the hall above he paused for a moment as if in doubt and then turned abruptly toward the west wing and, notwithstanding Stella's parting words, passed swiftly on until he reached the door of his "old quarters," then he drew a small, odd looking vial from his pocket and with it still in his hand, turned the handle and without word or warning, quietly entered the room.

CHAPTER IX.
MAURICE SINCLAIR ESCAPES WITH HIS VICTIM.

In the darkness of the night,
When the sun has lost command,
Wrong walks side by side with right—
Sin and truth go hand in hand.

Mrs. Sinclair rose late the next morning. A sleepless night had been followed by hours of heavy slumber which extended far into the forenoon. She awoke as she had retired, burdened with a trouble for which she could find no tangible form.

Here was her only son, resembling his father in face and manner,—a young man exemplary to all appearances, the knowledge of whose safe return, after long years of sorrowful separation, had overflowed her heart with gratitude and mother love, but whose actual presence thrilled her, not with unspeakable affection, but with an indefinable sensation of perplexity and apprehension. She blamed herself for the restraint which so evidently existed between Maurice and herself, and in this self accusing mood she rose and prepared earnestly to explore the seemingly inaccessible paths to her son's estranged affections.

Breakfast, was the first suggestion of her sensible mind. She smiled, even in her perplexity, at this prompting of the flesh, but obeying the practical impulse, she rang for the butler and assured herself that everything in this particular department was in its customary, excellent condition.

She was indeed perplexed and the limit of her logical nature was reached when she undertook the Herculean task of lifting the cloud which hung so heavily over her son's individuality. She saw no inherited trait, neither could she account for the developing of those peculiarities which so early in life branded her only son with the marks of evil associations and morbid desires. True, his faults at fifteen years were but the outcome of boyish adventures and experiments, but a nature like his, impulsive and so prone to investigation, had caused her, even in his childhood days, to look forward to serious, inevitable results unless added years brought more than the average amount of judgment to balance the opposing inclinations.

Living, as he evidently had, in ignorant and brutal Mongolian habitations, the seeds of vice, she reasoned, could easily have been fostered, yet why she should so persistently associate vice with every thought of this almost faultless young man, was a mystery she could not solve with all her reasoning.

She feared him intuitively, and with this thought of fear there came, strangely enough, a thought of Stella, and obeying an impulse which she could not resist, she went to the young girl's room to awake her for the breakfast hour. She knocked repeatedly at Stella's door, but there was no response. She called her name excitedly, then trembling with torturing apprehension, pushed open the door and entered the apartment.

Stella was not there. The bed was undisturbed, so also was each and every article about the room. Almost unconsciously she bent and picked up a small vial from the floor, and thrusting it into her pocket, rushed wildly into the hall and straight on to the rooms designed for her son's occupancy, and turning the latch without ceremony, stepped breathlessly in, only to find *that* also vacant and everything in perfect order. Running frantically about the house, for a few moments the bewildered woman forgot all self control and in agonizing tones enlisted every member of her household in a search for the missing ones.

All in vain: Stella and Maurice had disappeared in the blackness of the night, and the impenetrable fog had swallowed up their footsteps and obliterated every trace by which the direction of their flight could be determined.

CHAPTER X.
THE SCARLET HOUSE OF SIN.

The sinner stands with tearless eye
And looks on virtue's lovely grace:—
Too late, her soul's repentant cry
The brand of sin is on her face

At the very hour in the morning when Mrs. Sinclair and her servants were searching every nook and corner of the elegant residence, away over on the Surrey side of the great bridge, in a large brick house, standing far back from the street, two people, a man and a woman, were bending over a delicate form, clad in an evening dress of pure white satin that looked strangely out of place in this scarlet hued Harem of unchastity. The very hangings blushed in rose red symphonies for the sins and impurities of the inmates. The heavy carpet was one unbroken stain of blood red coloring. The daylight peered through the rich window drapings and crimsoned the entire apartment with its guilty glances within. The exterior of the house was dull, dark and uninviting, but within, the glare of crimson, of dull red and deeper garnet, blended in every article of furniture and garnished walls, ceilings and windows in bewildering and feverish arrangement. Even the glasses on the small jasper table by the couch were red with the evil light of their intoxicating contents.

The woman's dress was opened low at the throat and her jet black hair and clear olive skin were in sombre contrast to the clinging, reddish garment.

That the man had carefully disguised both voice and raiment was plainly evident, but that he was no stranger to the house or its extraordinary mistress, was also a self evident fact.

There were few who knew of this curious habitation, whose only furnishings were draperies and divans, small jasper tables and luxuriant couches, but the few who did were well content to contribute most generously for its maintenance, and more for the occupants of its numerous apartments, whose only glimpse of daylight was that which fell through the shamefaced windows and rested, like the hands of a bashful lover, upon charms, half strange and half familiar to his touch.

Julia Webber the mistress of this peculiar mansion, bent for a moment over the silent form, then she raised her eyes and looked with a strange, unseeing expression, into the wall beyond, as was her habit when addressing any one.

The voice was low and distinct, but as cold and unsympathetic as steel, as she said with hardly a movement of the lips, "Well what are your orders, Monsieur?"

The man at her side turned his eyes from the quiet face upon the couch and looked haughtily down upon her as he answered sharply, "The same as usual. Why do you ask?"

For an instant he caught the gleam of fire through her half closed, panther like eyes as she gave him a searching side glance to note the effect of her brief question.

"You decline my offer, then," she asked, even more coldly, more distinctly than before.

"What do I want with you?" the man exclaimed fiercely in excellent English. "Have I not told you, Julia, that my brief infatuation ended the hour that it began? Ah, she awakes!" he exclaimed suddenly, and bent lower over the prostrate girl.

Over Julia Webber's face there crept an ominous, ashen pallor. Her eyes blazed with the fury of a woman scorned, while her slender, jeweled fingers clutched the folds of her lurid garments with the grasp of a dying agony. Another moment and her emotions were controlled. The vindictive gleam in her eyes was unnoticed by the man, for at that moment his whole thought and attention was given to the white robed figure.

Stella, for it was she, opened her eyes and looked around the unfamiliar room in utter bewilderment. Then her gaze rested upon the young man's face, but without a shadow of recognition in the face.

With a smile of astonishing sweetness he bent gently over her and whispered softly, "Do not be frightened, Stella. You are safe with me. Rest a little and I will explain all."

Then, as her eyes closed once more in response to the powerful drug which he had administered, he turned roughly upon the woman at his side and bade her watch and wait upon this girl, then adding with a significant expression, "I make you responsible for her; I shall be back this evening;" he abruptly left the house.

When the door closed upon her companion, Julia Webber stood beside the couch, immovable as marble.

Her flowing garments slipped from her sloping shoulders until one half her bosom was exposed. The lines of her face were rigid, but the swelling bosom rose and fell in gasps that were almost convulsive.

Hatred, envy and revenge gleamed in her scintillating eye balls while she gazed upon the pure and beautiful features of Stella.

At last, through her tightly closed teeth she muttered, hoarsely, "So this is why he scorns me! For this girl of twenty. It is not her pretty face or perfect form in which lies her attraction for Monsieur, for I am equally beautiful, but it is her very virtue, her purity, that draws his passions like a powerful magnet and holds him her slave until the smirch of his own contamination is branded on her brow. Pah! These inconstant fiends; They mold us to their own ideals, then scorn the creature of their own admiring handiwork. But enough of this! My revenge must be as sweet as my disappointment is bitter. I am mistress here, and perhaps my gallant Monsieur, some other *more agreeable* connoisseur may sip the dew from your budding rose before you again enhale its fragrance.

"Ah, Captain, you here," she exclaimed as a stranger unceremoniously entered the apartment.

"How could I remain from your presence, my beautiful Julia?" responded the newcomer gallantly, then catching sight of the couch and its occupant he added, hastily, "My God! how beautiful! who is she and where did you get her?"

"Not so fast, Captain," said Julia, laughing quietly.

Curiously enough the handsome Captain's evident admiration for Stella evoked no jealousy in her heart, but was a source of satisfaction on the contrary.

Here was the opportunity for revenge on the man she loved, and she was not the woman to lose it, through any such foolish sentiment as that of jealousy. Revenge and love go hand in hand in such natures as Julia Webber's. Her life had been one long succession of conquests, but to one man only had she offered constancy.

Only those who are caught in the whirlpool of lascivious temptations can realize or appreciate the difficulty in fulfiling such a promise, but, Julia Webber, in spite of her evil life, was truer to a given word than many of her more righteous sisters. Her love had been accepted with alacrity, and spurned with contempt and loathing almost from the hour of consummation.

Now, as this thought again flitted through her mind, she turned to the destingue individual by her side, and answered playfully, "you know we tell no secrets here, Captain; she is here, and here to stay, that should be sufficient. She is slightly indisposed just now," she added, with a meaning smile, "but if you wish to see her—"

"I certainly do, Julia," and he also smiled significantly, as he eagerly awaited her reply.

The woman hesitated a moment, and then, apparently changing the subject, said archly, "By the way, Captain, there is a lovely crimson, velvet robe in Robinson's window—"

"You shall have it to-morrow, and then?" asked the Captain, anxiously—

"Ah, thank you, and, come in again to-morrow, Captain, I think I can arrange this little matter for you." Then she closed the door upon him, and again the panther-like gleam of her eye balls crept stealthily out between her half closed lids, but the smile that parted the thin red lips melted away in a heavy sigh, as she turned once more to look long and earnestly upon Stella's sleeping face.

CHAPTER XI.
JULIA WEBBER LAYS PLANS FOR REVENGE.

How poor the love that blindly seeks
To avenge the scorn its presence wakes,—
'Tis only smarting pride that speaks
A requiem, for its own mistakes.

Stella remained unconscious throughout the night, but she was carefully watched by Julia Webber, who would allow no one to enter the room where she lay.

She was bewildered and frightened when she awoke the next morning in such strange surroundings. During the night her dress had been removed and she was amazed to find herself robed in a long, comfortable garment of soft red silk, and by her side a slender table with a tempting breakfast on a dainty silver tray awaiting her pleasure.

When Julia Webber entered the room she went immediately to Stella's side and bending gracefully over her, touched her lips to Stella's brow, saying with the sweetest of smiles, "my dear child, I am so glad you are feeling better. I beg of you not to talk or distress yourself by fears regarding your safety, for I have already notified your friends of your whereabouts and you may be sure I will take the best of care of you until they arrive."

This falsehood fell so smoothly from the woman's lips that Stella, innocent and unsuspicious, actually smiled up into the lying face and whispered gratefully, "I know you will, my dear Madam, and I shall trust you implicitly. I cannot understand what has happened but I throw myself wholly upon your mercy and protection, and I know that I shall be safe in your hands."

Julia Webber's face was turned from the couch as she answered in a strange unnatural voice, "Try and sleep now and I will come in again soon," and as Stella obediently closed her eyes she went hurriedly from the room.

Although far better acquainted with her own remarkable nature than are mortals ordinarily, still Julia Webber could hardly understand her own emotions at this instant. Was it possible that she was considering for a moment a withdrawal of her schemes for revenge? She had promised this girl protection just as she had promised scores before, but the word protection had suddenly assumed a new definition in her mind. Hitherto it had simply signified safety from personal violence, from starvation or physical discomfort. Now it was suddenly assuming a new condition,—safety for chastity and virtue. Had she promised this? No! That was purely a personal matter, and what was more, she only allowed the temptation, she insisted upon nothing. But then, again, her methods admitted of no alternative. Her guests, as she had told the Captain, came "to stay," and time, temptation and constant warfare will win the bravest battle and conquer the most stubborn resistance.

Communing thus, she again returned to Stella's room and, standing silently by the couch, looked earnestly upon the girlish face.

Shouts of coarse laughter and snatches of careless song, together with the chink of glasses, reached her ear at intervals as she stood immovable in the quiet room, and involuntarily, with minute distinctness, the details of other admissions to her household were paraded slowly before her mental vision. She recalled the innocence of those rioting voices when they first fell upon her ear,—in nearly every instance uttering a prayer for their speedy return to home and loved ones, or casting themselves in supplicating despair upon her mercy. Her brain was filled to bursting with questions before unanswered, with possibilities before unconsidered, and moments sped rapidly by while she remained, mute and motionless, by the sleeping girl. Not a quiver of the eyelids betrayed the storm that was raging in her breast, but after a time she turned and walked noiselessly from the room.

She had decided,—and with Julia Webber to decide meant to act.

CHAPTER XII.
A SINFUL LOVE.

So closely love and passion blend—
Their limits we can not define—
One hardly knows they've reached the end
Until they've passed beyond the line.

To Mrs. Sinclair, Stella was lost indeed. Almost insane with grief, the good woman placed the matter in the competent hands of Scotland Yard, and closing her house to all visitors, gave herself up to a grief more bitter far than that which would be felt at death itself. She had at last discovered beyond dispute that her son had frequented the clubs and theatres of London for a year past, under different names and often in the company of a young girl, who, although evidently from the middle classes, was still sufficiently beautiful to attract the attention of casual observers and win the attention and preference of one so (presumably) fastidious as Maurice Sinclair.

This girl, she also learned, lived quietly with her grandparents on G— St., and was in all respects a most estimable young woman. Obtaining this information some two months after the disappearance of Maurice and Stella, Mrs. Sinclair went in person to the address given to ascertain, if possible, some further facts regarding her son's unrighteous past.

The house in G—St. looked deserted when Mrs. Sinclair's carriage stopped before its unpretending portals, but she was promptly admitted by a neat maid servant, to the presence of Elizabeth's aged grandparents. She found them mourning in pitiful grief the loss of their idolized grandchild, who they said had, according to newspaper accounts, committed suicide by jumping from the London Bridge on the very date corresponding to Maurice's appearance at his mother's home. They had identified the shawl which she had dropped from her shoulders, before taking the awful plunge into the river, and that was the only proof they had ever received, that their dear one's fate was the sleep that knows no waking.

Finding in Mrs. Sinclair a tearful, sympathetic listener, they gladly told her of Elizabeth's quiet, happy life with them; of her beauty and virtue, and from this emanated the story of Lawrence Maynard, the young lodger, and their belief that it was her unrequited love for him that drove her to the fatal act.

The young man was clever and handsome, the aged woman said. He wore a close cropped auburn beard, but his hair grew long, and lay in large, loose curls upon his forehead. He seemed quiet and steady, and seldom remained away from his rooms at night, particularly, after his apparent fondness for Elizabeth had been observed by them. No one had ever called upon him except a queer Chinese peddler who, he said, brought him rare and expensive substances for his chemical experiments. Between this man and himself, there was evidently a most satisfactory understanding. They had met first in China, and Elizabeth frequently stood and listened to their comical gibberish, while the Mongolian's beady eyes watched her with never failing interest.

There were times even when she fancied he looked anxiously at her, and once, when Mr. Maynard was absent, he tried with poor success to tell her something, but what that mysterious something was she could never ascertain.

Mr. Maynard had frequently warned them all against touching any of the test tubes, flasks, retorts and crucibles in his room, but evening after evening he called Elizabeth to watch the changing colors in the delicate fluids, or the crystillization of rare substances while he instructed her, so they honestly supposed, by many scientific and wonderful experiments.

This was all Mrs. Sinclair could learn from the aged mourners, and weary at heart she returned once more to her now cheerless home. She felt certain that this Lawrence Maynard and her son were one and the same person, but little did she dream of the actual facts that remained untold in the aged woman's innocent recital.

It was in this cleverly improvised laboratory that Elizabeth Merril, unknown to her feeble grandparents, passed the few deliriously happy hours of her otherwise unromantic life. She had entered in the full possession of her womanly dignity and virtue, only to become faint from the exhalations of tempting perfumes and intoxicated by the fascinations of the tempter's smile and passionate pleadings. Long and fiercely she struggled with her new born passion, but her lover's first, warm kiss drew her very heart from her bosom and almost insane with love and fear she twined her white arms around his neck and pleaded for his dear protection.

At last, in a moment of reckless passion, he consented to a private marriage only insisting on concealment of the same until he should give her permission to announce it.

A private marriage is but a compromise with virtue in every instance, but Elizabeth was young and inexperienced.

She trusted her lover implicitly, and although the affair was not as she in her girlish fancies desired, still it was a bondage of love and she would willingly have submitted to its chains until death if her lover had so commanded.

It was only the insurmountable difficulty of her condition that at last counteracted the mental and moral poison of his presence and broke completely the spell that his impassioned caresses had thrown so fatally about her.

When the truth burst upon her that concealment was no longer possible, she fled to his apartments and fell on her knees before him.

"Oh, Lawrie, Lawrie," she sobbed, "You must tell Grandma of our marriage, you must, or I am ruined!" and she wept as if her heart would break.

Then an awful fear seized upon her as she noticed the stern, defiant look that crept into his face at her words.

"Get up Lizzie" he answered, brutally. "You should have thought of this before. There," he exclaimed, throwing a paper at her feet, "there is your Marriage Certificate. It is false every word of it; our marriage was a mockery from beginning to end. Show the paper to your grandparents and clear yourself if you can,—I can do nothing for you."

White as death, Elizabeth staggered slowly to her feet, but no word escaped her lips.

For a moment man and woman looked into each other's eyes, then with a mocking smile Lawrence Maynard, her lover, her idol, her perjured husband, passed rapidly from the room.

Like one in a dream she bent and raised the paper from the ground, then with head erect and steady step she walked to her own small room and locking the door behind her, fell heavily upon the bed with the lying certificate clasped closely in her rigid hand. She awoke to the realization that he had wronged her, and before she could fairly endure that knowledge she realized that he had also deserted her, and from that time forth her misery was complete. Too proud to tell her weakness now in the hour of shame, she reasoned that death alone would erase the stain upon her character, and with this sole purpose forming in her half crazed brain she fled to the sluggish river and took the frightful plunge into its awful depths.

The fate of her supposed suicide had been chronicled, first by the descriptive reports of the bridge officers, at their respective stations, and secondly by the busy newspaper scribes who haunt police stations for the necessary matter to fill their allotted space in the columns of the various dailies.

Elizabeth, holding her babe on her arm, read the report of her supposed entrance to the great unknown world, on the very night of Mrs. Sinclair's visit to her grandparents and her own discharge from the Hospital, and smiling bitterly, she muttered to herself, "Yes, that is true. I am dead, dead and buried. Now nothing remains but the walking ghost of Lizzie Merril and" — here she looked sadly down upon the face of the sleeping child and added, "the mother of this innocent babe." Then she wrapped the shawl a nurse had given her, closer around the infant and hurried onward through the gloomy night:—whither she did not know.

Almost at that moment a young man turned the corner of the street and brushed past her, so near that his arm accidentally touched her shoulder. For a moment she stood perfectly still, then with a piercing cry, woman and child fell heavily forward and were caught in Maurice Sinclair's arms.

CHAPTER XIII.
THE CONTRACT BROKEN.

The weapon tempts her—see—she feels its edge—
Then breaks the contract—and returns the pledge.

The man whom Julia Webber addressed by the French appellation, Monsieur, returned that evening, true to his word. He was received with smiles by the mistress of the house, who told him, in all sincerity, of Stella's still unconscious condition, and urged him to wait a little before presenting himself to the bewildered girl. Steeped in the ways of evil and deceit as he was, still he discovered no treachery in Julia Webber's words, and departed somewhat reluctantly, but in perfect faith as to his ultimate success.

Julia Webber's desire for revenge was being fulfilled almost upon the hour of its conception.

It was now nearly noon of the day following Stella's entrance to her house, and yet the fascination of her new guest's presence was still strong upon her. She had decided upon her course of action during that period of outward calm and inward perturbation, while she stood beside the sleeper's unconscious form.

The silver clock in her private dressing-room was still tinkling the hour of noon when a maid entered and handed her a large parcel which had just arrived.

"Wait a moment, Jennie," her mistress said, and the extremely attractive maid, nothing loth to view the contents of the box, waited while the wrappings were removed and the magnificent robe of crimson velvet held admiringly to the light.

"Ask the young ladies to come in," was the next extraordinary command, and while she donned the exquisite garment, some seven or eight young women, strikingly beautiful in face and figure, filed noisily into the room, and threw themselves in graceful, negligent positions, upon the numerous couches and divans.

The robe was beautiful, and fitted her voluptuous form to perfection. After it had been duly admired and removed, the enthusiastic young women were horrified to see Julia Webber hold it from her at arms length while she lighted in succession a half dozen waxen matches and applied them in spots to the costly fabric. The velvet writhed and twisted, beneath the flame-like human flesh, whilst almost suffocating fumes pervaded every inch of the apartment. She held it thus in her hands, until it was completely ruined, leaving only enough uninjured, to show the original shape and beauty, then refolding it as best she could, she tied the wrappings again with her own hands and writing in large, clear letters across the package, "The Pledge of a Broken Contract," ordered her maid to return it at once, to Captain Carlisle, Hotel Victoria. Then she dismissed the wondering women and went once more to the room that had become so strangely interesting.

A moment later she stood beside the couch holding in her hand a cluster of delicious grapes, while Stella listened and ate with the expression of bewilderment gradually fading from her features.

"I wish you would tell me of yourself, freely and unreservedly," Julia Webber said, and Stella, realizing at last some degree of truth regarding this woman and her surroundings, was clever enough to know that innocence and helplessness were by far the best weapons with which to fight her cause.

In treachery and deceit, Stella was little versed, but as an intelligent and observing member of society, she knew only too well that they existed, and feeling altogether unequal to such a combat, she chose ignorance as the surest safeguard from further trouble.

It was Julia Webber's request, that she would not ask to leave this particular apartment, that first opened her eyes to the nature of her surroundings. She shuddered involuntarily as the knowledge forced itself upon her, but she noted, sadly, that in spite of that promise, the key was softly turned on the outside whenever her hostess left the room.

After a little thought, Stella concluded to tell her name, and the circumstances of her abduction as nearly as she could recall them, but it was only when she identified her abductor as Maurice Sinclair, and mentioned her relations towards himself and his lovely mother, that Julia Webber's face in any way betrayed her interest in the narrative.

"You say that you reside in this Maurice Sinclair's home," she repeated, excitedly.

"Yes," Stella answered.

"And he will inherit great wealth, unless you stand between him and his mother's affection, I infer," she continued more quietly.

"Ah, I had not thought of that," exclaimed Stella suddenly. "You must be right, that only could have been his motive for this awful deed. But I fear, so great is her love for me, that his plans will fail, unless I am safely restored to her."

"You shall return in safety," was the decided answer, while her listener's eyes blazed with the excitement of a new ambition. Here was her chance, and almost instantly her mode of action was decided. She had become sick and weary of her sinful life ever since that strange infatuation sprang up within her heart, and for one man's honest love, she would gladly have forsworn the admiration and homage of the world, but too late, she realized that man would never credit such as she, with honest love, and the scorn her tender sentiments evoked, filled her whole soul with bitterness and longing for revenge.

Now, through Stella's innocent and unsuspecting friendship, she felt the way was open for a more subtle and satisfying vengeance, and subduing her excitement with marvelous control, she continued seriously, "Miss Sinclair, the subject of my life and surroundings is not one that I should broach to you, but you have given me your confidence in a measure, and, believe me, you shall never regret it. Now it may be a bold thing for me to do, but I am going to ask you a question, and upon your answer will depend much more than you imagine. Have I your permission?"

"Certainly," was Stella's wondering reply.

"I wish to ask, Miss Sinclair, if I were to leave this place; abandon the life that I have led for ten years past and obey in future every regulation and restriction of respectable society, would you call me your friend and allow me to visit you at your home?"

For a moment only, Stella hesitated, then holding out her hand to this extraordinary woman, she responded sincerely, "forgive me for thinking of myself, but come with me from this terrible place and so long as your conscience can honestly claim my sisterly regard, it shall be yours."

The tears trembled on her long, dark lashes as she raised her eyes to Julia's face, but at that instant a rap sounded on the outer door and without replying, her companion rose and passed swiftly out into the hall.

The man whom she had known for several months only as "Monsieur" was standing in the wide, crimson draped hall, but the hangings were so thick that it was impossible to have overheard the conversation that had been carried on in low tones between the two.

Placing her hand upon his arm, Julia Webber led him without a word into the spacious parlor which was also draped, even more luxuriously than the other apartments, in costly fabrics of vivid scarlet.

Here she paused before him, looking into his eyes with orbs that blazed with anger, and through her tight drawn lips she fairly hissed the words, "Maurice Sinclair, your adopted sister has told me all. This is my house and beneath its roof you and she will never meet again."

Then, while he stood apparently amused at this new freak of a peculiar woman, she moved to a dainty desk, and filling out a check for many thousand pounds, signed it, and once more stepping before him, thrust it into his hand, saying calmly, "there is the amount which I have received from you. Now, go! and believe me, if you escape punishment at all other hands for your cowardly sins, the revenge of a woman's scorned devotion will at some time find you out."

Then, before he could utter a word of protest or amazement, he was left alone in the fiery glow of the blood-red parlor. He looked mechanically at the paper in his hand, tore it in half, and dropping it upon the rug at his feet, turned like one in a trance, and slowly left the house.

CHAPTER XIV.
IN CENTRAL PARK.

This life is a Drama, its Plot strange and deep—
We laugh at the Farce—at the Tragedy, weep:—
The acts are surprises—no waits intervene
And only the Author stands back of the scene.

For two months Sir Frederic Atherton had hardly eaten or slept, so great was his grief at Stella's disappearance. No stone had been left unturned by him in the search for Maurice Sinclair and his beautiful victim.

No shadow of doubt as to Stella's unspotted purity, crossed his noble soul, and in despair he sat down to a hasty breakfast at the Club, while he ransacked his brain to find, if possible, some untried scheme for Maurice's capture.

His eyes roved absently about the richly appointed place, and almost instantly, associated in his mind with these very surroundings, came the recollection of a former breakfast, at the same place some months previous.

He was breakfasting with a friend who had just returned from America, and in relating the news of their mutual acquaintances, mentioned the approaching reception of Mrs. Sinclair's adopted daughter.

Almost simultaneous with the mention of her name, a young man rose from another table and took a seat nearer the ones occupied by his friend and himself.

The young man was slight, but athlete in build, and his face, although dark and sunburned, would have been extremely pleasing, but for a suspiciously unnatural moustache, that drooped heavily over his mouth, completely hiding that feature and thereby seriously injuring the amiability of his expression.

The young man was evidently interested in their conversation, but Sir Frederic at the time gave it little thought, and the matter slipped from his mind a moment after. The occurrence returning to his memory so vividly at just this time, impressed him strangely.

Could this young man have been Maurice Sinclair, disguised and under an assumed name, masquerading about London, in search of information regarding his mother's household before returning thereto?

Then another idea, relative to the flight of Maurice and Stella, occurred to him, and suddenly springing to his feet he exclaimed excitedly, "I'll try it. It can do no harm." A week later he embarked *incog.* on a transatlantic steamer bound for New York.

Something seemed to tell him that Maurice Sinclair, hunted as he was by every police officer and detective in London, was sure, sooner or later, to fly to America for protection. Of course, the usual information had been cabled to American ports, but detection could be so easily avoided, that Sir Frederic felt that Maurice would take the risk as a choice between two evils. Then again he reasoned, that a man familiar, as Maurice was, with the ports of Hong Kong and Calcutta (and his blood ran cold at the very thought), would naturally return thereto if circumstances forced his departure from London. But obeying the whisper that had so plainly suggested America to his mind, he found himself, after a rapid passage, safely landed in New York, and shortly after, comfortably situated in the Brunswick, one of its most spacious hotels.

To a man like Sir Frederic, the encumbrance of an assumed name was a never ceasing annoyance. His was a nature wholly antagonistic to deception of any sort, but he knew that in this manner only could he outwit so clever a rascal as the one he was pursuing.

Fortunately, he found one true and tried friend before he had been in the city long, and together they worked and waited for clues that should lead to his loved one's speedy recovery. Weeks went by while he patiently searched, and four months after the disappearance of Stella, Sir Frederic, disgusted with his foolish chase across the water, was sadly preparing to return. On the last Sunday afternoon of his stay he went with his friend for a farewell drive through the magnificent boulevards of Central Park.

The day was perfect, and carriages of every description, from the private liveried turnout to the hired cab and rustic country wagon, were ambling along, filled with men, women and children, all bent on securing as much pure air and sunshine as was obtainable during the short afternoon. Suddenly, at a sharp turn of the carriage-road, the vehicle containing the two men came side to side with a light phaeton, whose diminutive pony was ably guided by an extremely stylish young lady, and there, sitting by her side in evident favor, was the man for whom Sir Frederic was searching and for whose apprehension all London was desirous.

CHAPTER XV.
DEATH.

Death overtakes us, one and all—
Oft times when life is at its best:
Before its fatal blade we fall
To deep and never ending, rest.

The two men recognized each other instantly, for Maurice, in his fancied security, had neglected the habitual disguise.

Quick as flash he snatched the lines from his companion's hands and struck the spirited pony a sharp blow with the slender whip.

Moments elapsed, however, before Sir Frederic could explain the situation to his friend and their stupid driver. Vehicles were constantly passing and when they were finally in readiness to pursue, the pony phaeton had vanished.

The necessary papers were secured after much trouble and expense and a description of Maurice Sinclair, as he now appeared, furnished the Detective Bureau, but all to no purpose. Maurice had again evaded capture.

The lady was readily found in one of the most fashionable homes on Fifth Avenue, but her information was limited. She denied that her companion was Maurice Sinclair, but that was of little consequence as it was more than probable he had adhered to the precaution of an assumed name, if nothing more.

For fear of further publicity, the parents of the young lady removed her promptly from the city, and another two months passed while Chicago, St. Louis and even the Pacific slope were thoroughly searched for the missing man.

At the end of that time Sir Frederic was forced to return to London by family matters and the search for his loved one was extended at every spare moment of his time.

Meanwhile, Stella was still a prisoner in that quiet house with its scarlet furnishings. In the entire time of her confinement she had never passed the threshold of her door or seen the faces of the other inmates whose voices reached her so indistinctly through the heavy hangings.

Julia Webber gave her every care and attention, but every entreaty for liberty was met with the same gentle but decided answer, "Wait, Miss Sinclair, — You and I will leave this place together, but my house must be empty, first."

Tired of questions that received no answers and prayers that were unavailing, Stella waited patiently and sadly for the hour of her release.

At last it came.

Julia Webber entered her room just at dusk one cold, foggy day and seating herself by her side, said seriously, "Miss Sinclair, I shall take you home to-night. We are alone now and I can close the house forever. Do not be surprised at my change in costume when I leave this place for it will never do for you to be seen in public with such as I. Your honor has been saved, now you must let me guard appearances as well."

Leaving Stella overcome with gratitude and happiness she left the room and going at once to her own boudoir, selected the poorest and plainest of her clothing and dressed herself modestly in a quiet grey gown, laying out at the same time another unassuming but far more costly robe for Stella's use. This she took to Stella's room.

After Stella was dressed for her long anticipated journey, she waited quietly in the spacious parlor while Julia Webber passed, for the last time, through the apartments of this magnificent, but extraordinary abode.

Everything was in perfect order.

Opening a secret drawer in her dressing-case, she took therefrom a folded paper and thrust it carelessly into a small leather bag that was suspended from her waist by a delicate silver chain.

Her money and jewels had been safely placed in the Bank some days before, and now she opened the wardrobe door and glanced curiously at the row of silken and velvet gowns, all costly and elaborately made, but each of some startling shade of lurid red.

For a moment only, she hesitated, then she closed and locked the door, turning her back resolutely upon it while she muttered bitterly, "I am done forever with that cursed color. What care I for man's homage, while my heart is breaking with the shame of unrequited love?" Then, as her eyes roved restlessly about the rooms, old associations arose within her, and obeying a sudden impulse of her reckless nature, she again had recourse to the waxen matches. This time it was the heavy hangings that she touched with the blazing tapers, and when she felt confident that the deed was safely done, she closed the door behind her and returning to Stella with a curious smile upon her lips, led her hastily from the house without a backward glance.

"Let us walk a little," she said to Stella. "It will do you good and we can take a hansom at the square," and so saying the two women walked rapidly along the foggy street while Stella's heart beat joyfully with this long desired accession to liberty and friends.

They had only gone a few blocks when an engine dashed wildly past them, its bell clanging frightfully, while the cry of "fire" was echoed frantically from every side.

Julia Webber smiled sadly and hurried on, almost dragging Stella in her haste to leave the excitement of whose origin she alone was cognizant, but as they rushed thus heedlessly, across the slippery street, a span of powerful black horses, frenzied by the clanging bell, rushed upon them in the darkness, and before the sturdy driver could control their maddened fury, both women were lying prostrate beneath the heavy hoofs.

CHAPTER XVI.
A DEER HUNT IN NEWFOUNDLAND.

How grandly beautiful the scene
Where ocean wrestles with its prey;—
The rugged rocks all fringed with green—
The iceberg glittering and serene—
And ocean, wearing both, away.

Away up on the northern coast of Newfoundland, in the month of September, a group of pleasure seeking tourists were idly lounging about a roaring fire, smoking and telling pleasing stories, while the aroma of good coffee, and an occasional whiff of savory venison steak wetted their appetites, and made them well pleased with themselves, the world in general and Newfoundland in particular. Only a short distance across the water they could see the smoke from the mining village of Pilley's Island, and hear the shrill whistle that called the swarthy miners to and from their labors in the cavernous drifts of an enormous mine of iron ore.

Sharks swam recklessly near their anchored craft, and seals protruded their shiny heads within easy vision.

Three pairs of enormous antlers spoke of their two days' sport, thus far, and enthusiasm was at its wildest among the merry hunters.

Only one man of the six who composed the party, seemed indifferent to the wild, untrammeled country; the possibilities of boundless wealth in the forbidden rocks, and the abundance of trout, seals, otter and deer that was to be had with little labor.

This man was Maurice Sinclair.

He had left London to save his liberty;—he had fled from New York on this pretext of pleasure for the same purpose, and now, while the others planned with great volubility the *modus operandi* of the day's sport, he was moodily thinking of the possibilities of life for him in the wilds of this half explored country.

Mining villages he dreaded, inasmuch as there was always danger of encountering some delegate from civilization—as the mining fraternity are of a nomadic tendency—and there was also the fear of the periodical steamer that conveyed the products of their labor to the States or Canadian markets. True, his sin had been that of abduction only, so far as the world knew, but "a guilty conscience needs no accusing," and Maurice Sinclair, although cleverly disguised, lived in daily fear of another and a worse crime being laid at his sinful door.

Under such mental strain it was not unnatural that the wondrous handiwork of nature, and the limitless possibilities for human advancement in this grandly beautiful region failed to excite his admiration or interest. The beauty of landscape; the sublimity of sky and ocean, inspired no sentiments of awe or appreciation in his debased and guilty soul.

At last all was in readiness for the anticipated sail up the picturesque bays, and Tommy Tully, a native hunter, whose services they had secured as guide and general entertainer, tapped him lightly on the arm while he stared with undisguised astonishment at so unenthusiastic a sportsman.

"It be your turn to-day, Sir," Tommy was saying, and taking the extended rifle, Maurice sprang lightly into the boat and with a smile accepted his position of honor in the prow.

According to Newfoundland game laws each stranger was allowed to shoot eight deer for the trifling sum of two hundred dollars, and as this amount, *per capita*, had been conscientiously paid down at the Crown Office in St. Johns, each sportsman took his turn at whatever game presented itself.

Tommy Tully was in himself a character typical of Newfoundland's choicest hunters. Tommy's experience dated back to the days when coraling deer was no unusual circumstance, and Tommy, in his own peculiar dialect, told them of once meeting an unusually large Buck, face to face, in a woodland path, unarmed and unexpectedly.

"He were too skeert to run an' so were I," said Tommy in conclusion. Knowing the Newfoundlander's adherence to superstitious faiths, the young men asked him with all gravity to relate some of the time honored traditions and prevailing beliefs regarding the uncanny "Fetch" and his nocturnal antics, and Tommy, nothing loth, regaled them with blood curdling recitals of white robed figures, half fish, half human, that skimmed the surface of the bay at midnight, searching with spirit lanterns for belated victims, and dropping his voice to a husky whisper, he continued, "jest over dis very spot, Sir, one night last summer, I stopped rowin' fer a bit to light my pipe and somet'in' riz my feet right up an' turned me clare roun' in de punt, jest hind side afore, Sir, never knowed what did it."

Just at that instant Tommy's eyes, which had, all through his narrative, been carefully scanning the opposite bank, glowed with excitement: His nostrils quivered and expanded like those of a keen scented animal, while with hardly a perceptible movement of the body he slackened the speed of the dainty craft, and then in a short, sharp, but carefully modulated voice, exclaimed "See him? Straight ahead,—Now! Fire!" But no report followed the order.

The huge antlers of the deer that had been plainly seen protruding from the dense thicket on the neighboring bank, trembled for a second as if their owner was undecided what course to pursue, then suddenly disappeared, and only the sound of crackling underbrush told of his enormous bounds through the apparently impenetrable forest.

The young men looked savagely at Maurice, as by an effort he threw off the spell that so completely enthralled him, and laughing pleasantly he passed the rifle to the next in turn, saying brightly, "Don't scold, Boys. The truth is, that fellow rattled me. I've lost my turn."

"And we've lost our supper, perhaps," they growled, rather savagely. But another look at Tommy's face silenced them.

Every muscle was alert with expectancy.

With skilful hand he guided the boat along, through narrow passes and wider openings, scanning the overgrown bank, and soon again his low toned order sent the excited blood tingling through their veins. "Now! Fire!"

This time a shot rang out sharp and clear upon the frosty air. A crash was heard in the thicket and rapidly bringing the boat as near an open space in the bank as possible, Tommy sprang ashore and dragged to the water's edge the most magnificent specimen of Caribeau they had thus far encountered.

"I knowed he'd hanker fer anudder look at us," muttered Tommy, gleefully. "Dere's a lot of springs in dem bushes and dose boys always knows where dere's good water."

Having acquired much expertness in their previous experiences, the *post mortem* operations were rapidly performed, and stowing away the desirable portions of the carcass in the "cuddy" the young men, now in thoroughly jovial mood, proceeded on their delightful excursion.

The obliging manner in which that particular deer had walked into rifle range was being joyfully discussed when an exclamation of delight broke from the lips of one of their number.

They were just crossing "Long Tickle," a narrow passage between two enormous hills of stone, and gazing outward the blue waters of the mighty ocean caught the eye, while far away on the very horizon there arose, seemingly to the azure heavens, a gigantic pyramid of ice, dazzling in its whiteness and reflecting with a thousand rays the glory of the morning sun.

The young men shivered involuntarily and drew their hunting jackets closer about them. They understood now the source of frosty breezes in the midst of genial sunlight and verdant foliage.

At "Hall's Bay Head" a wider glimpse of ocean was obtained, and Tommy noted with careful eye the "set" of the restless currents, while he told them of many instances where miners, rowing to their homes from the distant mining villages, had been caught in the treacherous tides at this place and carried far out to certain death upon the ocean, while the lights from their cottage homes were plainly visible on the rocky shore.

CHAPTER XVII.
BY THE ASHES OF A GUILTY HOUSE.

The voiceless ashes speak no word,

From the ruined walls no sound is heard,

But a cry of terror is in his ears,

And, lo, the ghost of his sin appears.

Restless and ill at ease, Maurice proved but a poor companion for those fun loving tourists. They had invited him, a chance acquaintance, on the strength of his gentlemanly exterior and genial bearing, but the change in his manner after they were fairly off, not only disappointed them, but in great measure dampened the ardor of what would otherwise have been a joyfully, hilarious party.

Therefore, it was with a feeling of positive relief that the unsuspecting youths saw him embark a little later, via Halifax, for his native shore.

They had visited the quaint little ports of Carbonear and Harbor Grace; crossed the turbulent waters of the Gulf, and after a brief stop at Prince Edward's Island continued their quest for pleasure through that most picturesque of all sections, the Brasd'or Lakes and Historic Arcadia, where the original home of Evangeline was pointed out to them by the ever patriotic natives.

Yet the oppression of an opposing influence was upon them and although Maurice's was but the sin of taciturnity and indifference, still it clouded their perfect enjoyment and threw a feeling of restraint over all their merriment.

For how can one be gay and joyful when one's companions are seemingly prostrate beneath the weight of unspoken anxieties?

It was a risky thing to do, to walk almost into the trap as Maurice was doing, but his was a nature that courted dangers and risks, a brief season of caution was always followed by some deed of extraordinary daring. Still, in this instance, Maurice had laid his plans with more than ordinary precaution.

It was now nearly eight months since the abduction, and Maurice knew well that even crime received but a brief share of attention in so vice laden a city as London. Nevertheless, he landed at Queenstown, and spent some time wandering about Ireland before he dared to brave the scrutiny of the lynx-eyed Scotland Yard detectives.

His first step on leaving Queenstown, was to secure a suitable disguise, and as his skin was tanned by exposure, and he now wore a heavy beard in place of the well shaven chin, he felt that he had little to fear. He reached London early in the evening, and proceeded at once to secure modest quarters in a quiet street.

From thence he sauntered out and was soon rattling over the stones in a hired hansom on his way to the well remembered house in Surrey. Whether he expected to find Stella and Julia still there, would be hard to guess, for his was a nature uninfluenced by surprises, but when he found, instead of the dark, unassuming house, nothing but a hideous pile of burnt and blackened timbers, a look of consternation *did* show itself upon his usually unruffled features.

What had been the fate of the beautiful girl whom he had left in perfect health and strength within these walls? Had she escaped, or were her ashes now mingling with the gruesome mass upon which the moon was casting such a melancholy light? He hardly knew what had prompted him to take this dismal drive, for he had not even dreamed of again entering Julia Webber's door. He knew, too well, that crimes committed beneath her roof were never allowed further circulation, and within Julia Webber's veins ran the blood of that hot-headed nation, where the Vendetta is perpetuated with true, religious zeal.

No, he had not dreamed of entering those forbidden precincts, and now, contempt for his own morbid curiosity filled his mind, and with a hasty order to the driver, he sank back once more upon the cushions of the comfortable conveyance.

Back to London he drove, looking out idly over the water as he crossed the bridge, but little dreaming that but for accidental aid, a human being would now be sleeping in the cold embrace of the sluggish river, and *that* crime, like many others, would be charged to his account in the day of divine reckoning. It is probable that if he had known and fully realized that fact, its realization would have made his expression none the less confident, or his indifference to his ultimate fate no whit less thorough.

Men like Maurice Sinclair, who chance the gravest issues of life, are more than glad to "trust to luck" their final venture into the great unknown, and the "fear and trembling" with which we are told "each to work out his own salvation," are conditions totally unknown to natures like theirs.

If he argued the matter at all, it was merely to say that the power that created the "inclinations of a man's heart evil from his youth" was also the power upon which all responsibility consequent upon those evil inclinations, should rest. Probably, he added, moreover, that a power capable of implanting evil in the heart of man could as readily have sown the seeds of good, and if evil was the seed, evil must have been the harvest sought. Thus, leaving out the human labor decreed for the gaining of salvations, he, like many others, shifted all responsibility and the possibilities of a mistaken theory never occurred to him.

He had not seen Elizabeth since the night when she and her child—her child and his—had fallen so unceremoniously into his arms on a windy street corner.

He remembered, without a blush, how he had cursed her when she begged for shelter, but finally, fearing she would follow and annoy him, he had taken her away down into Whitechapel, with whose vilest passages he was marvelously well acquainted, and there secured for her a miserable room, which she, being weary and sick at heart and having no alternative, was only too thankful to accept.

Another reason for this choice of location for Elizabeth's future home was due to the fact that a certain Mongolian, whose friendship he valued, was living in that particular vicinity.

This person he had known during his stay in China, but whether it was love or fear that bound them in such close alliance, would have been hard to determine from their conversation. At any rate the doings of each seemed well known to the other and each was equally pleased that it should so continue.

The mention of Whitechapel brought no terror to Elizabeth's heart, for, in the bitterness of her misery, uncongenial surroundings were of little consequence.

Strangely enough, the erring woman fears friends rather than strangers in the hour of her degradation. Whether it is that friendship rarely stands the test of sorrow and shame or any blow to its so-called pride, or whether the desperate courage which self abasement wakens in a woman's heart is a better safeguard for her broken spirit than the pity of her associates, I know not, but in nearly every instance an unfortunate woman will choose poverty and complete estrangement from the friends of her happier days rather than bear the scorn or their self righteous censure.

To the man who had so irretrievably wronged her, she clung with the pitiful persistency so frequently seen in those of her sex and now, as a passing thought of her fate entered Maurice's wandering mind, he suddenly became desirous of seeing her again.

Just then the hansom, which had been rolling along briskly over the smoother streets, came to a stop and "Cabby" leaning over, said briefly, "'Ere's the 'ouse you was haskin' for, Sir."

Maurice bent forward and once more found himself gazing upon Mrs. Sinclair's home in Portland Place. The windows were dark and not a sign of life was visible. "Strange," he muttered; "She would certainly have returned here if she had escaped." But during the full ten minutes that he remained before the house no sound within reached his ears, or no ray of light from its many windows told him of a living presence.

Convinced now that Stella's body rested beneath that hideous mass of blackened timbers and voiceless ashes, he sank back nervelessly upon the cushions and in a trembling, husky whisper, ordered the thoroughly puzzled driver to hurry on.

His last determination was to visit Elizabeth and to Whitechapel he was carried, with all the speed the overworked horses were capable of affording.

CHAPTER XVIII.
STELLA IS RESTORED TO HER LOVER.

When love illumines all the day
In which we changeful mortals live—
How swift our rancors pass away—
How doubly easy to forgive.

During the brief moment that the sturdy English driver succeeded in holding back that span of frightened horses, Sir Frederic Atherton sprang from the carriage and by almost superhuman strength, drew from under the threatening hoofs, one of the prostrate women.

A stalwart pedestrian ran to his assistance, but before the rescued woman could be placed out of harm's way, the other motionless form had been stamped upon and trodden into the earth by the infuriated brutes.

As soon as they could be controlled, Sir Frederic and the unknown man raised the slender form, but one glance into her quiet face showed plainly that her life was ended, and that death, even in so horrible a manner, had brought her peace and rest.

By this time, Lady Laura Trevor, Sir Frederic's sister, had alighted from the carriage, and learning the terrible circumstances, assisted her brother as best she could to place the two apparently lifeless forms within the carriage.

Not until Sir Frederic had taken the delicate form of Stella into his arms, did he receive any intimation of her identity. But as he laid her head carefully upon his shoulder, an indescribable feeling of fear and trembling passed over his manly form. It seemed as if the pain, the horror, and even the unconsciousness of the helpless girl was shared, by him. *Her* misfortune, for the instant racked *his* nerves with agony, and subsiding, dulled his senses almost to complete oblivion, and it was only with a vague feeling of amazement that he heard his sister's sudden exclamation.

The light of the carriage lamp had fallen on Stella's face, and although worn and pale from months of anxiety and imprisonment, it was readily recognized by Lady Trevor.

Her voice sounded afar off in Sir Frederic's ears, but pulling himself together with a great effort, he looked eagerly down into the pallid face. For a moment happiness overcame him and he held her to his heart in a perfect ecstasy of joy and gratitude, but in another instant, fear for the result of her injuries, usurped the place of joy and leaning from the window he ordered his man to drive directly to the home of his sister, which was near at hand.

The glow from the burning house reddened their way for some distance and fell with fitful glare upon the still, cold face that rested so heavily against Lady Trevor's arm.

Never was the sterling sense and philosophy of Mrs. Sinclair's nature put to severer test than when Sir Frederic led her, some hours later, into Lady Trevor's magnificent parlors, and she beheld, stretched upon ready sofas, the lifeless form of Julia Webber, and the apparently lifeless form of her long lost darling, Stella.

Controlling herself by a mighty will, Mrs. Sinclair watched and waited for the verdict of the famous physician, which should bring to her sorrowing heart renewed distress or unspeakable rejoicing. At last it came. Stella had raised her lustrous eyes to the physician's face, and then smiling faintly at Mrs. Sinclair, called her name, she nestled her hand in hers and fell back upon the pillow in a calm, recuperating sleep.

Meanwhile the dead girl had been laid with tender care in an adjoining room. In removing her tasteful garments Mrs. Sinclair unfastened the silver girdle and examined the contents of the leather bag to find, if possible, some clue to her identity.

The folded paper proved to be a memorandum of little consequence, but a brief statement of money deposited in a certain bank, gave them their only grain of information. This clue was acted upon at once, and both the body and the handwriting authentically identified thereby.

It was further ascertained that in this same bank the sum of one hundred thousand pounds, had been placed by her, and here also was found a will, drawn up and signed in perfectly valid form, bequeathing her entire property, in case of sudden death, to a prominent home for fallen women in the city.

With reverent hands they laid her in a velvet casket, and both Sir Frederic and Lady Trevor followed her to the tomb, while Mrs. Sinclair bent with joyful heart over the bedside of her cherished daughter.

Nothing was known at the bank of the character of Julia Webber's business.

The money had been deposited, little by little, for ten years, and left undisturbed until it reached a goodly figure, but during the ten years of her depositing they had never, in a single instance, cashed her check, and the eccentricity of their fair depositor, had caused much comment among the usually silent clerks.

It remained for Stella to reveal the evil of this woman's life and the source of her illgotten revenue. But woman's fame can never suffer in the hands of the innocent: only from evil thoughts, come evil speech, and in Stella's loving heart none but the kindest thoughts were ever entertained, and the sad death of Julia Webber, erased from her mind the last dark shadow of suspicion, and kept her memory forever faithful.

CHAPTER XIX.
SAFE IN THE ARMS OF LOVE.

Love, sacred love, how sweet thy will—
How perfect thy entrancing bliss—
What purer joy our hearts could thrill—
What rapture soothe our souls like this?

In a common cause of suffering or rejoicing, social distinction is frequently forgotten,—thus, over Stella's safe return friends, relatives and servants vied with one another in expressions of joy and gratitude, and even touched each other's hands in an outburst of heartfelt congratulation.

To Mrs. Sinclair, Stella related every detail of her most astonishing experience, and the tears she shed over Julia Webber's awful death were the proofs of genuine love and tender remembrance.

It is true that Julia Webber had insisted upon her imprisonment for eight long months, but from what had she not saved her!

Of Maurice's whereabouts she knew as little as did Mrs. Sinclair, and after the first recital his name was never mentioned between them. To her faithful friend, Sir Frederic Atherton, Mrs. Sinclair repeated Stella's story, but between the two no mention of the matter was ever made.

In her perfect innocence, it never occurred to Stella that her imprisonment in Julia Webber's house was anything more than unfortunate and humiliating, and if any more disagreeable thought entered Sir Frederic's mind it was promptly banished as an unworthy suggestion of a worldly education.

During the weeks of convalescence through which Stella passed after the shock of that evening's disaster, Mrs. Sinclair scarcely left her side. The two were inseparable, and during the long winter evenings they would sit before the blazing, open fire, which was always to be found in Mrs. Sinclair's cosy sitting-room on chilly nights, Mrs. Sinclair in the comfortable rocker with Stella's golden head pillowed lovingly upon her knee, while the young girl sat in graceful comfort on the heavy hearth-rug, or a convenient ottoman.

The sorrowful days had left their traces on Mrs. Sinclair's raven locks, and in the shadows about her eyes, but an expression of supreme thankfulness shone on her face as her eyes rested lovingly on Stella's wavy hair. Only now and then when silence fell upon the air, the sweet mouth curved in lines of sadness, and her motherly eyes seemed trying to pierce the clouds of uncertainty and apprehension that closed around her at every unfamiliar step or voice.

It was as if she looked and listened for a nameless something while she dreaded its coming with a mighty dread. Even now, when a card was handed her by the servant, her hand shook perceptibly as she took it from the salver. A look reassured her, and smiling into Stella's upturned face, she said, "It is Sir Frederic, love, shall we have him right up here?"

"Certainly, mamma if you wish," was the simple response, but in some way the face that a moment before was demure and white as the lily, is now flushed and brimming with joy like the heart of an opening rose.

Rising, she had only time to seat herself decorously on the comfortable sofa when Sir Frederic entered.

"Ah, Sir Frederic, I am more than glad to see you this evening," said Mrs. Sinclair, as she gave him her hand in greeting.

"And I," responded he, "have been counting the moments since dinner in my eagerness to come and yet not presume upon your hospitality by the earliness of my appearance."

Then turning, he continued with a sudden rush of tenderness in his tones, "and you, Miss Stella, are glad to see me?" He was so absorbed in the contemplation of her face and his eagerness to hear her answer, that Mrs. Sinclair's somewhat unceremonious exit from the room was unnoticed.

Stella smiled, and giving him her hand, said softly, "I am very glad, Sir Frederic, it is always a pleasure to see you, but to-night,"—here her eyes filled with tears, "is the anniversary of all our trouble, and you have been our best and dearest friend, mamma's and mine. I don't know what we should have done without you," here her voice grew fainter as she continued, brokenly, "I don't know what I,"—

She could not go on, and Sir Frederic, placing his arm tenderly about her, pillowed her head upon his breast while he whispered gently, "You shall never do without me again, little one, for indeed I cannot live longer without you. I may not tell my love prettily, Stella, for I am little versed in that pleasing art, but if a life of untiring devotion can speak my love, I will gladly give you that. Look up dear heart, and tell me that you will give yourself to me forever."

But Stella did not look up. Instead, she nestled her head deeper in his arms, but as his lips touched her shining hair, he murmured with a satisfied and radiant smile, "my darling, my wife."

To a man of forty who has lived his life unsinged by passion's blaze, and unblinded by young love's delusion, the blessing of a woman's love brings peace and happiness, almost too great for human understanding. All the currents of his soul go out to her, and the restless rivers of his mighty nature find peace at last in the unfathomable ocean of her love.

Thus it was during the first sweet hour of their betrothal. In Sir Frederic's heart the calm of a great joy followed like a summer cloud upon the path of a sorrowful tempest.

Not so with Stella, however, for with the first great rush of joy on knowing that she was so beloved, her very identity, past, present and future, seemed lost in his. A glorious panorama of heavenly sights and entrancing music burst upon her vision.

Self was lost in the whirlpool of future joys and duties, and the only object that stood clear before her eyes was the form of her heart's beloved, and to him she clung with all the fond abandon of her simple trusting nature.

Body and soul she gave herself to her lover, as woman can only give herself once in the period of her existence, and in deeply reverential spirit, Sir Frederic received the precious gift and cherished it forever.

It was Mrs. Sinclair's voice at the door that at last recalled the lovers to a vague consideration of things earthly.

The eyes of an indifferent observer could hardly have misunderstood the situation, and Mrs. Sinclair only glanced into Stella's face and in another second her darling was in her arms and both were laughing and crying in true woman fashion.

CHAPTER XX.
DR. SEWARD'S EXPERIMENT.

Our bodies are only an instrument clever
By which the soul works out a phase of existence—
Each member responds when the soul moves the lever
Unless overcome by abnormal resistance.

Ever since the morning that Lady Van Tyne confided her belief in Maurice Sinclair's Satanic individuality to her family physician, the remorseful Dr. Seward was imbued with an undying curiosity to learn more of this human phenomenon. But the abduction of Stella, coming so suddenly upon them, made it almost impossible to indulge his interest in that direction.

Naturally he would not care to mention the subject to the grief tortured mother, and as to Lady Van Tyne, her excitement rendered her totally incoherent whenever the subject was broached. Another reason for sensitiveness on the part of Dr. Seward, when in the presence of Mrs. Sinclair, may have lain in the knowledge of his guilty secret, the unburdening of which, would have been to press the dregs of shame to Lady Van Tyne's lips and pierce the devoted mourner of Archibald Sinclair where her love and faith were tenderest. Thus it was not until after the restoration of Stella to her foster mother's arms that the impatient physician learned ought of the young man in whom he had taken so unaccountable an interest.

It was now some time after Stella's recovery and Dr. Seward was sitting, for a brief social call, with Mrs. Sinclair in her pleasant parlor. Dr. Seward had been a faithful friend for years and now that her darling was safe, Mrs. Sinclair told him freely of Stella's unfortunate experience and of the information which she received of her son during her brief call upon Elizabeth Merril's grandparents.

The old physician was deeply interested in the narrative and made occasional notes on one of his visiting cards in reference to the matter. The names of Lawrence Maynard and Elizabeth Merril were heavily underscored and the card placed carefully in his pocket.

The doctor laid great weight upon the absence of intuitive, motherly affection in Mrs. Sinclair's case at her son's appearance when she had clearly explained her feelings to her old adviser, but she only saw in his rigid cross questioning the life long habit of scientific analysis and gave little thought to the problem which the physician was trying, in his clever brain, to solve. More interested than he cared to admit, Dr. Seward only waited a few days before going to G— — St., as had Mrs. Sinclair before him.

The aged couple, burdened with sorrow, were only waiting the hour when, hand in hand, they should enter the dark valley of the shadow of death, even as they had walked through the many checkered paths of a life of nearly four score years.

Perhaps it was a mercy that their trusting hearts were spared the actual knowledge of Elizabeth's fate, as the sweet memory of her childhood and girlish days was always a solace even in their moments of grief. Could they have seen her at any time during the year that had now elapsed since her disappearance, the misery and squalor of her surroundings and the shame of her one error, would have occasioned their virtuous souls far more anguish than the awful death which they supposed to have been her fate. Calmly, and with unvarying precision, the white haired woman related to Dr. Seward the only crumbs of information it had been her lot to gain, and from another room she brought a small, oddly shaped vial, containing a dark brown powder, which she said she had found in his apartments when her eccentric, young lodger had left.

The vial was without a label and heedful of Mr. Maynard's frequent warnings the cork had never been removed.

It took but a glance to show Dr. Seward that it was an exact counterpart of the one found in Stella's room the morning after her abduction, and placing it carefully in his pocket he took kindly leave of the aged people, and not wholly dissatisfied with his morning's work, returned speedily to his private office. It was about three in the afternoon when he seated himself in his easy chair, and adjusting his glasses prepared to examine, from a purely analytical standpoint, the brownish powder contained in the little vial. He held it to the light, but it was opaque, dull and uninteresting. He shook it, but the agitated particles fell back as indifferently as possible to their original positions. Then, true to his vocation, he removed the stopper gingerly between his first and middle fingers and raised the vial cautiously to a respectful distance from his nose. The first sniff was entirely non-committal. The next was a little stronger effort and he thought he detected a faint, sickish odor.

Shaking the bottle again gently, he drew it nearer and took a bold inspiration immediately over its contents. Almost instantly his hand fell to his side; the vial fell upon the heavy carpet, spilling most of its contents, and these, as they came in contact with the air, ignited and burnt, while the sickening, penetrating fumes arose like incense and completely filled the spacious apartment. For one hour by the clock he sat there, motionless as death, but fully cognizant of all that passed about him. He longed, with true scientific fervor, to rescue the vial with its remaining contents, but his members were benumbed and motionless. He heard the signs of life in and about the house, but was powerless to raise his voice. He even fancied, in his speculative manner, that he was experiencing the sensations of a disembodied soul after the resurrection, and his scepticism regarding spiritualism and theosophy, was shaken to its very foundation.

There was no terror in the situation and almost from force of long trained habit, he noted every symptom of his condition with great precision and detail. He saw the hands move slowly on the clock before him, and felt the draught from a half closed door blowing softly upon his back. This trifling matter amused him, coming to his mind, as it did, in the midst of grave, spiritualistic meditations, and the mental smile which accompanied the amusement was another proof of the absolute uselessness of the fleshy body for all demonstrations of like nature.

It seemed strange to him that he had never before realized how useless an encumbrance the body was, after all. He could see, hear, smell and think, and his mind conveyed him wheresoever he willed, so that really only the power of speech was denied him. Suddenly it occurred to him that speech also was possible, but it must necessarily be a communion of similar disembodied souls rather than intercourse with ordinary mortals, and while he was longing with all the zeal of his investigatory nature for an opportunity to test his mental vocabulary, a tingling sensation began in his extremities and passed, almost like an electric current, through all his members. His living death was ended, and concentrating all his energies, he staggered from the chair.

The fumes from the burning powder were now exhausted, and bending unsteadily, he secured the half emptied vial and corking it firmly, concealed it once more in his pocket.

Then touching an electric bell, he sent a peal vibrating through the house, and a moment later, when the frightened assistant hurriedly entered, it was only to find the good physician stretched in apparently dreamless slumber upon the office sofa.

CHAPTER XXI.
A PERFECT UNION.

A happy marriage is, in truth, a lovely thing—
A forest of perfect joy from which all virtues spring.

The months of another year flew swiftly by and still nothing was heard of Maurice Sinclair. It was finally concluded by all that he had escaped to some foreign port and the search was finally abandoned.

In her new joy, Stella overlooked the past as only youth can overlook its sorrows, but in Mrs. Sinclair's heart there was always a bitter pain and a mother's prayer for her erring boy.

It was the second anniversary of that never to be forgotten ball, but it was Stella's wish that the crowning happiness of her life should take place on the recurrence of that night which brought them all so much of grief and misery, and, although torn with varied emotions, Mrs. Sinclair was well content that it should be.

Thus, in the grand drawing room of her foster mother's home, Stella and Sir Frederic were married.

The ceremony was strictly private, as the shadow of sin and sorrow still hung heavily above their heads.

But to Stella it was as the glorious dawn of another life, whose anticipated pleasures were far in excess of any she had heretofore experienced. Peace and joy spread their white wings about her and the haven of her husband's love seemed the very portals of Heaven itself.

For this night also, the shadows were lifted from Mrs. Sinclair's face, and banishing with a resolute will, the fears and anxieties of the past, she entertained the few guests with her old time gracious stateliness.

As for Sir Frederic, it mattered little to him that the world was full of sorrow; that every pleasure came attended with more or less of grief and pain; that rogues and rascals exceeded by far the honest members of society and all on earth was vanity and vexation of spirit. Into his life had come a bliss, capable in itself of turning bitter, sweet; of overcoming evil with good and changing all the darker passions of life, chameleon like, beneath the rays of his rosy lenses.

It was Stella's own wish that they, Mrs. Sinclair, her husband and herself, should visit America on their wedding journey, and Sir Frederic, thinking it would be best for them all to leave for a time the scenes of so much sorrow, readily acceded to her wish. Not but that he would have consented just as readily to a trip across the Sahara or to some unexplored region in the mountains of the moon, but America was her wish, and to America they sailed on the first Cunarder that left Liverpool after their marriage.

Stella's marriage to Sir Frederic, although a quiet and unostentatious event, brought, both to Stella and Mrs. Sinclair, a sense of security and protection that was very grateful after the anxieties and excitement of the past.

Women may prate of independent self reliance, and scorn the assistance of man during their hours of success and pleasure, but seldom it is in the darker days, when danger threatens and the weakness of a delicate organism assumes alarming proportions, that the willing hand and steady head of an honorable man, goes unappreciated.

Goodly numbers there be, whose only claim to manliness lies in body and garments, from the weakness of whose intellects, brave women turn with ill concealed disgust, but an unwomanly woman it is that does not value true masculine strength and bravery and turn with grateful heart to the protecting arm that is proffered so gladly in each and every disaster of life.

It seemed to Stella that forever and ever she was safe from the temptations and evils of life, and upon the rock of her husband's protection she threw herself with that tender helplessness so dear to an adoring husband's heart.

Woman has done much to increase man's femininety by her persistency in doing his duties for him, and if now her "lord and master" sits calmly by while she labors for the support of the family, the responsibility of this deplorable result rests, in nearly every instance, upon herself or some other self-sufficient member of her short sighted sisterhood.

Mrs. Sinclair had been an almost worshiping wife, but her independent nature responded to the touch of necessity, and in the time of required bravery no woman could have acted with greater courage and judgment.

Thus, in Stella's childlike trust, Sir Frederic recognized the germs of noble womanhood, and respect and reverence blended deeply with his tender love and passion.

When at last the service was ended and man and wife were clasped in each other's arms, that measure of perfect and enduring love was felt by them that is rarely known in this world of thoughtless and misguided unions.

Little did they dream that on the very night of their perfect happiness, another terrible tragedy was being enacted, with Maurice Sinclair in the villain's role and Elizabeth Merril again the victim.

CHAPTER XXII.
"QUEEN LIZ."

A cry in the darkness—a crime in the night.—
With the blood of the victim the sharp blade is wet;
In silence we gaze on the horrible sight—
The dark deed is done—but the end is not yet.

It was on this very night that the habitues of that particular passage in the Whitechapel section, gazed with sentiments of mingled awe and curiosity, as Sam Hop Lee withdrew the bloody weapon from the prostrate body of "Queen Liz."

Elizabeth's reputation in the passage was pretty clearly defined in our opening chapter. Her ability to defend herself and friends against her pugilistic and plundering neighbors had been the eventual outcome of fear, desperation and the first law of nature.

She shunned their society from the first, and acting on the advice of one who knew the ways of rogues and rascals from long association, she demonstrated her skill in the use of "protecting irons" at the very first provocation. Jealousy and envy surrounded her, yet so great was their fear of genuine bravery that Elizabeth managed to live pretty much as she wished in her own wretched room. She guarded her beautiful baby girl with the ferocious affection of a tigress. Not an instant, day or night, was the child allowed out of her sight so great was her distrust of those by whom she was surrounded.

But in some way from the first, Sam Lee had in many ways befriended her. He had given the baby queer little chop sticks to play with and not infrequently an odd looking paper of curious tasting tea was slipped into her hand by the beady-eyed mongolian. Recognizing him at once as Mr. Maynard's mysterious peddler, Elizabeth was inclined to be suspicious of his friendship, but as days and weeks rolled by she found herself going oftener and oftener to his quarters, and never in a single instance did he abuse her neighborly advances. She tried hard to teach him the English language, but in spite of his earnest efforts he proved but an indifferent scholar.

Soon it was noticed that the genteel looking stranger who spent so much time with Queen Liz, became also much at home in the Chinaman's shanty, and they were frequently heard conversing in that peculiarly abbreviated language that was so bewildering to those who listened.

The genteel stranger was always arrayed in a heavy coat with a jaunty cape and a soft felt hat slouched suspiciously over his eyes. His beard was red and closely cropped, while a tawny moustache completely concealed his mouth. He was seldom seen during the day, but partook strongly of the habits of the other residents in his nocturnal goings and comings.

Queen Liz always escorted him safely to the street, and it was observed by the more curious that her face wore a happier expression after one of his visits, and her whole manner betokened a lighter heart. She would fondle and caress the baby, which she always kept spotlessly clean, and occasionally her voice was heard as she sang some plaintive air to the uncertain accompaniment of a clanging Chinese cymbal.

But to-night it was all over, and as Sam Lee withdrew the glittering knife from her bleeding side, a terrible frown darkened his brow; Chinese curses and lamentations followed one upon another, and to the bewildered spectators it seemed as if, in his own heathenish method, Sam Lee was swearing vengeance on the murderer, whom he had evidently recognized by the weapon. At any rate, he removed the woman and the child, and the inmates, nothing loth, resigned all claim upon them both, and soon the episode, like many others of similar nature, was forgotten.

Only a week later the Chinaman's shanty was closed and no one of the trio, Queen Liz, the child or their benefactor, was ever again seen by the inhabitants of the passage.

CHAPTER XXIII.
ELIZABETH FINDS FRIENDS.

He who has suffered knows the pain,
That other sufferers bear;
And from the torn and bleeding heart,
Flows balm for every care.

The first day at sea was fair and uneventful, but on the second day a curious episode occurred upon the deck.

An under-officer, young and with a frank, boyish face, came quietly, hat in hand, to where Mrs. Sinclair, Sir Frederic and Stella were sitting, and in a respectful manner requested permission to address the ladies in behalf of a poor woman and her child who had shipped in the steerage.

The woman, he said, was refined in her appearance, and was very seriously ill while her sufferings were necessarily aggravated by her incommodious surroundings.

With a modest blush he went on to say that ever since he discovered her wretched condition he had been scanning the faces of the passengers in search of a kindly heart and had finally decided upon their party as the one most liable to assist him in his humane undertaking.

She was being cared for, in a measure, by a kind hearted Mongolian, but his sympathies were won, not so much by the woman as by the baby, who seemed almost entirely neglected.

He had learned that the woman was a victim of intended murder, and the Chinaman whose name was registered among the steerage lists as Sam Hop Lee, had taken both woman and child and gone forth unaided and unasked, in search of the murderer whose face he knew and who he had good reason to believe, was now in New York.

The story seemed plausible, and the memory of their own bitter sorrows fresh in their minds, made their hearts ache with sympathy in the poor woman's behalf, still, quite naturally, the ladies hesitated before taking upon themselves so great a responsibility.

But the young officer, with a shrewd knowledge of women's hearts, ran forward, and as quickly returned with one of the "sweetest, cunningest babies in the world."

At least, that was the verdict of both ladies on the very instant of the little girl's appearance.

The baby settled the matter, as the young officer almost knew she would. She looked into Stella's lovely face and smiled, but she opened her little arms to Mrs. Sinclair and nestled her curly head in her motherly arms and no coaxing or inducements could alter her decision. Fortunately, a berth was secured for the invalid, but no one ever guessed that it was the young officer's own stateroom that was so promptly offered for her acceptance.

Sir Frederic made many attempts to gain more information regarding the unfortunate woman and her child from Sam Hop Lee, but his limited English so confused and muddled him that there was little satisfaction to be gained.

The young officer succeeded better through a slight knowledge of the Chinese tongue, but whether Sam Lee did not sufficiently understand or whether he had some reason for remaining silent it was difficult to determine.

However it was, nothing definite was learned through repeated conversations with him, and he gradually slipped back to his position in the steerage and the ladies saw no more of him during the voyage. The woman was suffering, not only from an incisive cut in the side, just over the lower rib, but also from an obstinate attack of pleurisy from exposure and lack of care, so that conversation with her was, at the time, impossible.

The little girl was sweet and affectionate and soon made friends with all on deck, much to the satisfaction of the young officer who, apparently, looked upon her as a sort of protégé.

Little did Stella and Mrs. Sinclair dream of the disclosures that time was destined to reveal regarding this innocent child and her unhappy young mother.

But before another day had passed, a story was brought to their wondering ears that made them forget for a time the sorrows of others in the extraordinary development of their own life tragedy.

CHAPTER XXIV.
STELLA CONFIDES IN HER HUSBAND.

The sky is dark with storm and cloud—
The ocean's face is cold and drear—
But deep within two loving hearts
The light of faith burns ever clear.

The steamer was now about half way across the Atlantic, and this was the first disagreeable weather she had encountered. To-night the wind blew heavily; the waves rolled high and few of the many passengers remained on deck after the "dog watch" was set.

Mrs. Sinclair felt a slight sensation of that much dreaded and truly awful malady which bears the mild, delusive name of sea-sickness, and remained quietly in her berth, but Stella, clinging to her husband's arm, reached a somewhat sheltered spot on deck, and there, with his arm about her, Sir Frederic sat and looked about over the fast darkening ocean.

Clouds, black and threatening, were rolling heavily across the sky, while the winds howled angrily through the rigging, and the white capped waves threw themselves against the steamer's sides as though enraged at her stubborn resistance of their destroying wills. Truly, sky and ocean, air and space, seemed joining powers in a mighty effort to overthrow the universe, and were only lashed into greater fury at the defiance cast in their very teeth by the handiwork of man. Yet the steamer advanced steadily forward, coquetting with the gentler waves and breasting the more determined ones with dogged persistence.

But to Stella, the confusion of the elements brought only a feeling of greater security in her husband's love. She looked to him and trusted; she clung to him and was safe,—for come weal or woe, they were together, and death by whatever manner could bring no terror, so that it found her in his arms. After a few moments of silent contemplation, Stella raised her eyes and whispered softly, "Dearest, there is something I would like to tell you, in fact, I should have done so before but I was so happy I dreaded to revive old memories,—but now, I feel that I would like to tell you, of that night—"

"No, Darling," Sir Frederic interrupted, quickly. "Do not speak of it Stella. Try and forget all that is past, and live only in the joys of the present and future," and he pressed her closer to his side as if the joy of *his* present was sufficient to eradicate all memories of unpleasant nature.

"But I think I would feel easier if I could tell you, dear," she pleaded. "It was all so strange, but neither you or mamma ever asked me and some way I have never felt like mentioning it myself until to-night. Do let me tell you, Frederic," she entreated.

"Stella, dear, if you wish to, certainly my love, only do not let your memory dwell upon so painful a subject."

"It is about that night," Stella said softly. "I had gone to my room to retire, after telling Maurice plainly which room I was to occupy. I closed my door and threw open the window for a moment while I stood, injudiciously you will say, and let the damp mists cool my face. I did not hear my door open, neither did I hear his step, but suddenly a most peculiar odor stifled me. I turned quickly to see from whence it came, and there was Maurice standing by my side. The expression on his face was horrible. I opened my lips, involuntarily, to scream, but no sound came. Instead, my throat and lungs seemed instantly filled to suffocating with the stifling odor. I grew dizzy and would have fallen but he caught me in his arms. Then he wrapped my cloak about me, — put my traveling cap on my head, and, Frederic, I walked out of the room with his aid, through the hall to the side door and actually entered a cab, knowing all the time exactly as well what I was doing as I know now, but it was impossible for me to speak or think connectedly. I could not move without his aid. So it was throughout that long and dreadful ride; I could neither speak or move but I heard and understood every word that he addressed to me. He evidently knew the exact nature of the drug that he had employed for he talked to me all the way, telling me his plans, and the awful fate that awaited me if I did not yield to his wishes. But this I must say to his credit, that in no way did he molest me and I was as free from the pollution of his touch when I left the carriage as when I entered it."

Here Stella's voice died away as a specially vindictive gust swept by their sheltered nook, and Sir Frederic, after pressing a tender kiss upon her lips, sprang to his feet and wrapping her closer in his ample rug, almost carried her across the deck and down to the comfortable stateroom, then leaving her with Mrs. Sinclair, he climbed the stairs once more, and walked back and forth across the slippery planks, trying to calm, if possible, the tumult of indignation and sorrow, that Stella's recital aroused within his breast.

Soon two other passengers joined him in his solitary walk, and it was evident to him by the peculiar roll of the body, that one of the newcomers at least, was well accustomed to pacing slippery decks and encountering heavy seas. Sure enough, he was the old "sea dog" whose genial, brown face had won the hearts of all at the Captain's table. He was Commander of some ship now on dry dock, and was taking this opportunity to try a voyage with his friend, the Captain of the Cunarder.

To-night, he had succeeded in enticing a particularly timid young man on deck to "try the weather and brace him up a bit," as he good-naturedly explained it. But now that he was once more walking the deck in the teeth of a "rattling breeze," 'his cup of pleasure overflowed and he proceeded to terrify the young man nearly out of his wits by a thrilling sea yarn of earlier days.

Sir Frederic, realizing that a story told on deck is common property, linked his arm in the young man's unoccupied one and catching step as best he could, walked on, while he listened somewhat absently to the Captain's narrative.

CHAPTER XXV.
THE CAPTAIN'S STORY.

What manner of mankind is he
Who dares impersonate the dead?
Alas! The doom of treachery
Must some day fall upon his head.

"It was twelve years ago," the Captain was saying, "and I was in charge of the 'Water Sprite,' running from Liverpool to Calcutta. She was a rakish little craft, with a slippery keel,—quick to mind her helm and would carry sail to the last, but we'd had a long, rough voyage and all hands was pretty nigh used up, but when we was about three days from the eastern port we was struck, almost unawares, by a terrible gale. I say unawares, but I must own we was in pretty good shape for squalls all the time, but on this partic'lar night I staid below more'n I should if it hadn't been that one of the young chaps that shipped 'tween decks in the cargo at Liverpool, was a dyin' out of pure out and out sea sickness.

"Well, as I was sayin; the first officer was on the bridge and I was sittin' below with young Sinclair, when"—

"Excuse me, Captain,—Sinclair, did you say?" exclaimed Sir Frederic, suddenly aroused to interest by the familiar name.

"Aye, Aye, Sir, Maurice Sinclair, a lad of about fifteen years. He said he'd got into some scrape at home and had just started out on his own hook, and"—

"Maurice Sinclair,—Twelve years ago,—Did he die?" Sir Frederic almost screamed in the old Captain's ear as a howling blast swept by, nearly driving their feet from under them.

The old man steadied him with a powerful hand but his ire was rising at these frequent interruptions to his favorite yarn, and he answered somewhat snappishly, "Die? Yes, poor lad. He died in my arms that very night in the height of the gale, when the rigging was swept away and the waves was washing the upper deck—"

"Can you prove that?" demanded Sir Frederic, excitedly.

"Prove what? that the rigging was swept away?" thundered the old salt, now thoroughly angry.

"No! No!—that Maurice Sinclair died in your arms, twelve years ago."

Well I ruther guess I can, seein' as I've got the young chap's partin' letter to his mother in London and a picter of the old lady herself"—

"Let me see it, quick," said Sir Frederic, then in a measure controlling himself, he told him as briefly as possible of Maurice Sinclair's return to his mother's house a little over two years ago and of the crime for which he was wanted by the city authorities.

The old Captain was inclined to be incredulous, but before Sir Frederic had finished his story, his ire had vanished, so also had all recollection of the yarn he had been about to spin, and leaving the timid young man to return as best he could, he laid his hand on Sir Frederic's arm and hurried him down the companion way while he muttered spitefully between his teeth:

"It's a lie. Maurice Sinclair is dead, and that rascal, whoever he is, is a Damned Imposter!"

CHAPTER XXVI.
SORROW AND REJOICING.

The pain of death hath bitterness
Too deep for man to name —
But, ah! the poignant sting of grief
Accompanied with shame!

Words can hardly convey the feelings of wonder, sorrow and relief that followed each other in rapid succession through Mrs. Sinclair's mind at the old Captain's story.

She looked upon the undeniable proof of her own photograph with tears of thankfulness in her eyes, while the last repentant words of her only child, brought pain too deep for utterance or demonstration. It seemed that two lads of about the same age, strangers to each other, became inspired with the mutual desire to run away from parental authority and try their luck upon the ocean.

Neither of the lads dreamed for an instant that their unexpected entree into the Captain's family, when they were safely out of port, would be greeted with less than cheers and congratulations, or that other than ease and glory would be their portion for the remainder of the voyage.

Fortunately, for the success of their expectations, the Commander of the "Water Sprite" had a gentle heart under his rough exterior, and moreover, had boys of his own at home, so he only insisted on their earning their glory by keeping the brass work shining and allowed them to eat their fill at the second table.

The boys were singularly alike in feature but widely different in expression and disposition, Maurice being mischievous and happy, while Jack Fenton, the other lad, was ill-natured and vicious in his dealings with his companion in the adventure.

On the day preceding the terrible storm, Maurice was taken violently ill, and notwithstanding all was done that could be under such limited circumstances, he passed away almost at the very moment, when, rudderless and with her rigging swept away, the "Water Sprite" drifted helplessly at the mercy of wind and wave.

They were all saved through the timely assistance of an outgoing steamer, but Maurice's dead body was left to find a watery grave, through sheer inability to remove it.

The other lad was safely landed in Calcutta, and the Captain soon lost track of him in the press of his many duties.

To the old Captain, Maurice had told much of his home surroundings and the letter to his mother, on the day of his death, was written at his instigation, when his experienced eye saw that the black shadow was fast settling down upon the frail lad's features. Before he died he gave his ring, his clothing and the few other trifles that he had managed to conceal about him when leaving home, to his comrade, Jack Fenton.

Afterward the Captain regretted that he had not retained these treasures with the photograph and letter, but years passed by and in the varied excitements and dangers of his adventurous life the incident was only remembered in connection with the terrible disaster to his favorite vessel, but the letter and picture had traveled about with him for twelve long years, so safely hidden in the case of his miniature pocket compass that their very existence was forgotten until the moment of Sir Frederic's astounding revelation. The night was far spent before he had finished his narrative and answered the almost innumerable questions of his excited hearers.

They little heeded the violence of the storm, so great was the tempest of sorrow and rejoicing that raged within their hearts. When morning broke, the ladies were more composed, and a peaceful smile rested upon Mrs. Sinclair's face.

Truly, the grief for a loved one whom death has taken from our hearts and homes, is nothing in comparison to the shame and sorrow for one upon whom evil deeds have left an ineffaceable stigma. A load seemed lifted from her heart and although sorrow fell like a pall around her, still the bitterness had been removed and even in her bereavement she could find great cause for heartfelt thankfulness.

The sick woman was slowly recovering and the little Elsa was like a ray of sunshine, lighting up each grief darkened heart with her merry prattle.

Promptly upon their arrival in New York the suffering woman was placed in the wards of St. Luke's Hospital, but the little girl was gladly retained under the watchful eye of motherly Mrs. Sinclair.

Some way, in the bustle and confusion of disembarking, Sam Lee was totally forgotten, but the beady eyes of the Mongolian watched their every movement and in his own quiet way he soon discovered the destination of both the woman and the little girl.

It was not long before Sir Frederic secured the lease of a handsomely furnished house, and removed, not only Mrs. Sinclair and Stella, but also the now convalescent woman and her child, to this beautiful, although transient, home.

CHAPTER XXVII.
THE MARRIAGE CERTIFICATE.

The chain goes on in endless round,
Its motions slow or fast—
But every link is firmly bound
Twixt present and the past.

For several days after his experiment with that little vial Dr. Seward was too ill to more than raise his head from the pillow. He was a large, portly man and the continued nausea from that sickish odor completely prostrated him.

He would not disclose the cause of his illness to any one, consequently the wildest rumors floated about among his friends and patients and almost every affliction in the calendar, from apoplexy to measles, was ascribed to him. Weeks passed and, although fully restored to health, the sensations he had experienced could never be quite erased from his memory, and although he frequently awoke in the morning with the grim determination to again examine that brownish powder, night invariably found him as ignorant of its constituents as a good, wholesome fear could make him.

In a moment of almost unprecedented mischief he labeled the bottle with the words "Death to the Inquisitive" and laid it carefully away in a private drawer.

But now that Stella and Sir Frederic was married and they and Mrs. Sinclair were so happily settled over across the water, his desire to penetrate the mystery of Maurice Sinclair's identity returned with all its force.

The bottle was his only clue and that a very unsatisfactory one, as the one found in Stella's room was empty when discovered. He could not compare the contents, so what was the use of risking another journey to the land of spirits, he argued.

But at last science prevailed, and determined not to again defy the enemy alone, he put the vial in his pocket and ordering his carriage drove swiftly to Guy's Hospital to ask the assistance of his friend, the Superintendent of that Institution, in his perilous undertaking. Dr. Seward related to his friend the particulars of his first experiment and with the unassuming vial between them, they consulted long and earnestly on the best method of attack.

The powder was inflammable in air and must therefore be protected. The first step was to test its solubility, so drawing a small quantity of water from the Burette into an Erhlenmeyer flask, Dr. Seward carefully removed the cork and placing the necks of the two bottles together succeeded in shaking a small quantity of the powder into the water. Then the vial was recorked and set carefully away. The powder did not dissolve and the experimenter waved the flask gently back and forth over the flame of a Bunsen burner while his friend retired to another room to complete a little experiment that he was working on when Dr. Seward arrived.

A moment after, he reentered holding a smoking tube in each hand.

"Well how is it?" he enquired, interestedly, as he looked about anxiously for a stand to place his test tubes in.

"Insoluble in water," was the answer as Dr. Seward held the flask to the light and scrutinized the particles which were floating, apparently uninjured, in the almost boiling water.

"See here, Doctor," said the Superintendent desperately, "You have more hands than I, just now; Do you mind stepping into the office and bringing me that paper on reactions? You will find it right in my desk."

Dr. Seward rose immediately and passed into the office. Standing by the open desk with the flask raised high in one hand, with the other he turned over a pile of papers in the somewhat disordered receptacle.

At last he saw one, wrinkled and stained, and feeling sure that its demoralized condition was received through the spatters from an evaporating dish or the careless handling of re-agents, only, he unfolded it, and shaking his glasses down upon his nose by a clever movement of the head, glanced carefully over its contents.

"Can't you find it?" called his friend from the Laboratory.

But Dr. Seward did not answer.

The Superintendent found his tube stand, and depositing his work in safety, started for the office to assist in the search for the required paper. The two men met in the doorway. For an instant the amazed Superintendent thought his staid and venerable friend had taken leave of his senses, or that the unknown substance he was analyzing had developed some heretofore undiscovered ingredient and the excitement of Dr. Seward's face was promptly reflected on his own.

"What is it?" he asked excitedly,—"What has happened?"

"Where did you get that?" was the doctor's extraordinary reply as he held before his eyes a stained and wrinkled Marriage Certificate.

"That?" said the Superintendent, "let's see, where did I get that?" and he took the paper in his hand and glanced thoughtfully over its contents.

"Ah,—I remember, the Gardener found it by the front gate a year or two ago and I saved it thinking I would try and find the owner, but some way, it has slipped my mind altogether. But why are you so interested?" he asked, suddenly. "Do you know the parties?"

"I think I do," was Dr. Seward's reply. "Let me take this for a day or two, Doctor," he said, "and I may be able to clear up a sad mystery by means of it."

"Certainly, but come, tell me about it. You have aroused my curiosity."

Thinking there could be no harm, the physician told him the entire story only leaving out his suspicions and Lady Van Tyne's name from the narrative altogether.

The Superintendent was greatly interested, and as the same Gardener was still employed on the premises, he sent for him and requested the particulars of the discovery and the date as near as he could recall it.

Fortunately, as another matter of more importance to the Gardener occurred on the very day of his finding the paper, he was able to readily supply the exact date, and reference to the Hospital books showed plainly that a young women, enceinte and unconscious, had been found by Dr. Jennings and admitted to the wards that same morning.

One of the nurses recalled her perfectly and mentioned the fact of her being drenched to the skin when found. Her description of the young woman tallied exactly with the picture of Elizabeth Merril which the Doctor had seen at the house in G—— St. Remembering that the only clue upon which the supposed suicide had been identified, was the finding of her shawl upon the bridge, he questioned the nurse further and ascertained the fact that the suffering woman was without a shawl and that the nurse had herself provided one on the afternoon of the patient's departure.

Satisfied that Elizabeth Merril was not only an injured wife and mother, but a living, suffering woman, the now thoroughly interested physician took possession of the paper, and after ascertaining the whereabouts of the officiating clergyman by means of a directory, drove immediately to his address.

The analysis of the brownish powder was for the time forgotten.

Dr. Seward had little difficulty in finding the reverend gentleman of his search, and as briefly as possible he explained his errand, then laying the water stained paper before him, he waited with almost bated breath for the proof of its validity.

CHAPTER XXVIII.
TOO LATE.

Too late—their sorrow now is o'er—
Their trusting hearts have ceased to beat;
Beyond the clouds their spirits soar
To Heaven's beautiful retreat.

The clergyman was gray and bent with age, and it was some time before his feeble sight could discover a corresponding entry in his private memorandum book of marriages. At last he found it, and Dr. Seward stooped and read, in the old rector's handwriting, the brief statement of a marriage contract between one Lawrence Maynard and Elizabeth Louisa Merril, the date corresponding to the one on the wrinkled certificate.

To make matters even surer, the two walked slowly across the street and entering the gloomy doorway of a small, stone paved Chapel, passed on into the vestry and carefully examined the record of events occurring within its walls.

Again their search was successful.

Elizabeth Merril had been a lawful, wedded wife for nearly three years, and deep in thought as to what course it was best to pursue, Dr. Seward took leave of the venerable churchman and proceeded slowly on his way to the home of the aged couple in G— — St.

He was as undecided how to act when he at last stood before the quiet house as he had been when he left the Chapel, but as he ascended the steps an exclamation of dismay escaped his lips.

From the old fashioned brass knocker on the door there fell an ominous fold of black crepe, and before he could fairly recover from the shock of its appearance, the door was opened from the inside and a prominent lawyer of his acquaintance extended his hand and drew him into the narrow hall.

"Just in time, Dr. Seward," said the lawyer in a subdued voice. "I was about to send for you; Mrs. Merril has passed away and her husband is fast following her. I have just drawn up his will and appointed you joint administrator with myself in the settlement of his small estate. He begged me to suggest some one and you were the first to enter my mind. Don't refuse, old fellow, for the man is dying and there is no time to look further if the matter is to be arranged before his death."

Confused, regarding his duty in the matter, Dr. Seward entered the chamber of death, but his practiced eye saw plainly that the information regarding Elizabeth came too late to be understood by the suffering man.

The will was rapidly signed and sealed, and as if only waiting to complete this final act, the grey haired man turned feebly on his pillow and closing his eyes, passed painlessly from life to death, as had his devoted companion a few short hours before.

The funeral service was ended, and with uncovered heads, both Dr. Seward and the friendly lawyer stood beside the new made graves in the little cemetery.

Their duty to the dead was over, and now, as arm in arm they retraced their steps to the silent house, Dr. Seward again related the particulars of Elizabeth Merril's disappearance and his subsequent discoveries, while the astute lawyer, bristling with legal eagerness, listened and drew silent conclusions from the physician's limited stock of information.

The purport of the simple will was as follows:—

The sum of five thousand pounds, together with the house in G— — St., with its furnishings, were to be kept in trust for their missing granddaughter, Elizabeth Merril, in case the reports of her death should prove unfounded, but if at the end of ten years no trace of her could be discovered, both house and money were subject to the wills and dispositions of the worthy lawyer and physician who were made joint administrators by this last will and testament of the deceased.

Almost certain that Elizabeth Merril or Maynard still lived, the lawyer promptly undertook the difficult matter of finding and restoring her, as rightful heir, to the modest possessions of her lamented grandparents.

Meanwhile, Dr. Seward, acting upon a much desired plan, made prompt arrangements for an extended vacation, and great was the surprise in his mechanical household when he announced his intention of visiting America.

He felt that Sir Frederic and Mrs. Sinclair should be consulted at once regarding the secret marriage, so placing the valuable paper in his steamer trunk, he boarded the fleetest greyhound and was soon far away upon his long anticipated journey across the Atlantic.

CHAPTER XXIX.
THE HOME IN NEW YORK.

'Tis woman's best and sweetest claim
To bear the honored name of Wife—
But oh, how often is that name
Her bitterest trial throughout life.

It was evening, and the cosy parlor was bathed in rosy light, the curtains were drawn, and true to their old time customs Mrs. Sinclair and Stella were seated in easy chairs before a glowing fire.

Stella did not sit at Mrs. Sinclair's feet as she did a few months ago; oh, no, now she sat in the matronly dignity of her months of wifehood in the rocker by Mrs. Sinclair's side, while her husband, quite forgetful of his newly acquired position, was well content to lie at her feet on the heavy rug and look admiringly up at her lovely face, while little Elsa romped and tumbled about the room and turned things generally topsy-turvy in the exuberance of her spirits.

Mrs. Morris, little Elsa's sweet faced mother, seldom sat with the family during these peaceful evenings, although both Stella and Mrs. Sinclair had frequently urged her to do so.

She had insisted on performing the lighter duties of the house, and Mrs. Sinclair, appreciating her sensitiveness on the subject, persuaded Stella to allow her this as the surest means of keeping her beneath their care and influence.

Not a question had been asked her regarding the past, as in Mrs. Sinclair's just opinions, the sin of inquisitiveness overbalances in nearly every instance the blessing of charity.

With tears in her eyes she had requested them to call her Mrs. Morris, admitting that it was not her name, but before she could say more, Stella had placed her arm about her and whispered encouragingly, "You need tell us nothing; trust in us as we shall in you, and try and feel happy in our home and I know there will be better days to come. I, too, have suffered, but you see how radiantly happy I am now," and laughing from the very overflowing of her joyous heart, Stella kissed her tenderly and bade her speak no more on the subject.

Dr. Seward's arrival surprised them greatly, and now, as they sat around the blazing fire they listened eagerly for the news which he hastened to relate. He told them of his visit to G—— St. and his examination of the powder, describing his feelings as nearly as possible while under the control of that peculiar drug; and now that Stella had so thoroughly overcome her horror of the subject, she also described her experience and corroborated the physician's vivid description in every particular. Not until he told them of Lawrence Maynard's secret marriage, did they relate in turn, the details of Maurice Sinclair's death as revealed to them by the story of the old Commander.

The physician was completely overwhelmed for a moment at this seeming verification of his own suspicions. He had felt instinctively from the first that the man who so completely upset the Lady Van Tyne's composure on the evening of his first appearance, was not the son of Mrs. Archibald Sinclair, yet now, in the presence of the unsuspecting woman, the bewildered Doctor was speechless and disturbed.

At last he felt it necessary to continue the recital, and rallying his wits he congratulated them sincerely on their fortunate information and the proof that had so stubbornly denied all possibility of error.

With sorrow for the misguided girl, they glanced curiously over the certificate and Stella, rising a moment later to adjust the shade, laid the paper carefully upon the nearest table.

While they were still talking, the portieres dividing the double parlors were pulled gently aside and Mrs. Morris entered in search of the little one, as it was long after her usual hour for retiring.

Stella immediately introduced them, but for a moment Dr. Stewart nearly forgot his manners in the piercing scrutiny of his glance. Somewhere he had seen that face before, or one resembling it closely, but ransack his memory as he would, he could not recall the circumstances.

Turning quickly from the physician's searching gaze, Mrs. Morris said softly, "come Elsa, come to mamma; it is high time little girls were safely in bed!"

But Elsa was hiding beside Mrs. Sinclair's chair, and that good lady, with a face as demure as possible, was aiding the little culprit in her mischief by holding a fold of her gown about the tiny figure.

Mrs. Morris saw the playful ruse and stepped across the room to pull the little one from her hiding place, but in doing so she had to pass the table and quite accidentally her glance fell upon the paper which Stella had just laid down.

For a moment she stood and stared as if she could hardly believe her senses, then with a sudden bound, she seized the paper, crying, "Oh, my certificate, my certificate! Where did you find it?"

It was several seconds before any one spoke.

The little one crept from her hiding place and looked with wondering eyes upon her mother, while the woman, realizing that now all secrecy was over, turned pale and looked from one to the other with an expression of piteous pleading in her eyes.

It was Mrs. Sinclair who was first to recover from the painful surprise. Rising hastily, she placed her arm about the trembling woman, saying in tones of sympathy and tenderness,—"My dear child, is it possible that you are Lawrence Maynard's wife?"

"No, no," almost screamed the woman, as she shrank from Mrs. Sinclair's gentle touch. "I was not his wife, but do pray believe me, I honestly thought I was!" and she fell upon the floor, cowering at Mrs. Sinclair's feet in the humiliation of her shame.

Not till her words of self immolation reached their ears, did any one present dream of the possibility of her ignorance regarding the validity of her marriage, but now Dr. Seward sprang to his feet and lifted her tenderly from the carpet to a sofa, while he explained as clearly as possible, the result of his investigations.

"My poor girl," he said gently, "why are you so distressed? Is it possible that you have been deceived in this matter? You are indeed the lawful wife of Lawrence Maynard. I have proven the validity of that marriage by the clergyman himself. There is no reason why you should not look us all in the face, and with your help we shall soon be able to probe this matter to the bottom."

For a few moments Elizabeth could hardly believe the welcome words. She looked eagerly from one to the other for confirmation of the blessed fact, then, as her eyes rested finally upon her baby's face, she fell upon her knees at Mrs. Sinclair's feet and sobbed for very happiness.

As quietly as possible, Stella rose, and taking little Elsa in her arms, carried her gently from the room and out of the sound of her mother's hysterical weeping.

CHAPTER XXX.
SAM LEE DISCOVERS A FARO GAME.

A hard thing it is to recall to another
The seeds of wrong doing our brother has sown
But harder it is, our proud spirits to smother
And confess to a harvest so largely our own.

It was long past midnight before the ladies thought of retiring, so great was the excitement consequent upon the evening's revelations. But at last the Doctor and Sir Frederic were left alone. The fire was growing dim, but neither of the gentlemen thought to have it replenished. The physician's mind was so intent upon the identity of Lawrence Maynard that it seemed at last to react with unconscious cerebration upon the thoughts of Sir Frederic, for he paced the room thoughtfully a few moments, then pausing directly before his companion, said anxiously, "Dr. Seward, have you any theory whatever regarding this man, — this imposter?"

Like one confronted by the utterance of his own private thoughts Dr. Seward started and was for a moment embarrassed, but controlling himself, he said briefly, "Yes, Sir Frederic, I have a theory, but it is so vague and so intensely disagreeable that I dread to give it utterance."

Then, as Sir Frederic turned away without further questioning, he too, rose excitedly and began pacing the floor.

"Sir Frederic I *will* tell you my suspicion," he said suddenly, after a short silence. "It may be but a foolish fancy, yet I cannot shake it off." Then he told him fully, but with deep remorse, of the episode in his early life in which the Lady Van Tyne figured so conspicuously, but with the determination to shield his patient to the last, he told the entire story without mentioning a name, still to make his theory well founded, he was obliged to state that the two boys were as alike as brothers, and Sir Frederic, with a sinking heart, gave a shrewd guess as to the children's parentage.

He was only a few years younger than the Lady Van Tyne and he now recalled many instances of her imprudent demeanor when a girl, but the reflection cast upon Archibald Sinclair's morality by the Doctor's story, was a source of deep regret when he thought of the patient, still worshiping, wife.

In another moment his mode of action was decided, and placing his hand upon Dr. Seward's shoulder, he said sadly, "Doctor, I will respect your story as I have no doubt as to the truth of the facts you have stated, but unless this matter can be handled without one word of her husband's treachery coming to Mrs. Sinclair's ears, I shall quietly withdraw from the search and allow that masquerading rascal to go 'scot free,' so far as I am personally concerned."

"And I will gladly close my lips," answered Dr. Seward, "if you so advise, but find him, we must, for it is more than possible that my suspicions are unfounded and I can never rest until the matter is settled."

Sir Frederic had no time to reply, for after a hurried rap upon the door, the portly butler, red with excitement, entered, and beckoning Sir Frederic aside, said apologetically:

"There's a Chinaman down at the basement door that says 'e must see you hat once, Sir! I hordered 'im away, but 'twas no use. 'E says 'e's bound and determined to see you!"

Sir Frederic had not seen Sam Lee since the day of his arrival in the city, but he recalled him instantly, and feeling sure that *his* was an errand of importance, he dismissed the indignant butler and listened with great eagerness for what the Mongolian had to say.

Sam Lee had improved his time while in New York and could now communicate quite fluently in his funny, broken English, but now, in the intensity of his emotions, his newly acquired learning forsook him and for at least five minutes he poured forth a succession of abbreviated words and sentences that were positively maddening to a man so seriously interested as was Sir Frederic.

But at last he seemed to comprehend the situation, and ceasing his voluble chatter, repeated, over and over again the words, "Me find him! Me find him! Melican man come klick, — Chinaman show way!"

Sir Frederic, sure that the words were true, motioned for Sam Lee to wait and then ran back to the parlor where he hurriedly explained the news to the physician and requested him to act his pleasure about accompanying him on so disagreeable an errand.

Dr. Seward was eager to go, and in a few seconds both men were ready for the street.

Thinking Stella might be alarmed at his protracted absence, Sir Frederic mounted the stairs and turned the latch of her sleeping room as softly as possible.

The light was burning dimly, and as he surmised, his wife was far in the land of dreams. Her fair hair fell upon the pillow, while the coverlid, slipping from her shoulders, exposed her tender loveliness, and almost with tears in his eyes, Sir Frederic bent and touched his lips to a wandering curl while he covered the dimpled shoulders, and then with another look at the beautiful, childish face, turned and passed noiselessly from the room. The thought that his fair and innocent darling had once been held within the power of this unprincipled villain, sent his blood tingling through his veins, and with a sudden thirst for vengeance in his soul, he quickly rejoined the others, and following closely upon the heels of the excited Chinaman, was, an hour later, in the actual presence of the man who for nearly three years had succeeded in evading justice and escaping the penalty of his guilty deeds.

CHAPTER XXXI.
CLEVERLY CAUGHT.

The game of chance is played by all—
The rich, the poor, the great, the small;
Fate's hand the wheel of fortune drives,
And marks the epoch of our lives.

The street was one of the shortest in the city, extending only the one block from Broadway to the Bowery, and the house itself was plain, dark and unattractive, but Sam Lee led the way with an ease that betokened much familiarity with the neighborhood.

Sir Frederic had thought it best to enlist the services of a detective and now the four men entered the narrow hall and ascended a flight of stairs as noiselessly as possible.

Sam Lee was still ahead, and arriving at the door above, he gave three short, sharp raps, following these with a peculiar double knock that could hardly be mistaken if once heard. Evidently the signal was so well given that the wary watchman within did not doubt the friendship of the executor and neglected to open the wicket as was his usual custom before admitting any one. Instead, he opened the door a tiny bit while he put his eye cautiously to the crack, but before he could get a satisfactory glimpse of the new comers, Sam Lee's heavy, cork soled shoe was forced into the narrow opening and four stalwart, determined shoulders were braced against the door with a force that sent the careless watchman spinning backward across the dimly lighted passage.

There were seven or eight men in the inner room when they entered, but in less time than it takes to tell they had all disappeared but one, and he, too, would have vanished had not Sam Lee darted into his very arms and screamed like a parrot in his unintelligible gibberish. As quick as flash, Sir Frederic and the detective grasped the rambler's arms, but after the first wild rush, he made no attempt to escape but stood silently before them as if surprised, but in no way alarmed, at their somewhat extraordinary proceedings.

"This can not be the man," said Sir Frederic, doubtfully.

"Yes! Yes! Me know him!" yelled Sam Lee, over and over, while he held to the victim's coat tails with a grasp of vengeance.

"We will soon see," said the detective, grimly, as without ceremony he pulled both hat and hair from his prisoner's head.

With a movement as quick as lightning the man's hand flew back to his pistol pocket and in another moment the detective would, in all probability, have fallen, shot through the heart, had not Sam Lee, who was still holding fast to the coat observed the rapid movement and seized the would be murderer's arm with his wiry fingers. An awful struggle followed. As if knowing well it was his last chance for life and liberty, the man fought fiercely, with the strength of a lion, but he was finally held and the all conquering irons snapped upon his wrists. Then the false beard was removed and once more Sir Frederic looked upon the face of Maurice Sinclair as he had seen him upon the evening of that memorable reception. Older and more haggard he looked beneath the light of the rusty chandelier, and rascal though he was, Sir Frederic felt a thrill of pity for the reckless nature that should bring its owner to such bitter degradation. Sir Frederic was the last to leave the room and, as he reached the door, he looked again to note more accurately the nature of the place.

Faro, seemed to be the inducement, and that the game was well patronized was evident by the quantity of bills and silver strewn recklessly about the floor during the precipitate retreat of the players.

Not a soul was visible when they descended the narrow stairs, and save for the perpetual chatter of Sam Lee, no word was spoken during the short walk that brought the prisoner within the protecting walls of Police Headquarters. Whether or no the Mongolian's chatter was understood by the silent prisoner could not be determined, for once only, did he betray the slightest interest in his talk. Sam Lee had evidently referred to some incident of the past, as the word "Calcutta" was plainly recognized, and although the look accompanying his words was dark and threatening, the effect upon the handcuffed man was only to make him throw his head back and laugh long and heartily, as if well pleased at the untimely recollection.

Not until he heard that laugh did Sir Frederic really believe in his prisoner's identity. He had heard that musical, ringing laugh once before in Mrs. Sinclair's parlor and now he was certain there was no mistake. After seeing their charge safely guarded, Sir Frederic and Dr. Seward left their cards and promised to supply all further information the following day.

Sam Lee's dark face was still contorted with painful memories, and as the three men rode slowly homeward, Sir Frederic tried to ascertain the wrong which he felt positive the Chinaman had suffered at the hands of the man they had just left. He learned enough from the broken English to prove his vague surmise correct, for the words, "Calcutta Sister," and "Revenge" were only too suggestive of the nature of Sam Lee's grievance. "Sam Lee wait and wait," he said, "some time get revenge," and then with the same warning shadow upon his face, he bade them set him down at a quiet corner, and the two friends, sympathizing deeply with his unmistakable sorrow, shook his taper fingers and drove rapidly homeward.

CHAPTER XXXII.
FACE TO FACE.

Is it cruel remorse that now palsies his members.
And burns in his eye balls like fierce, glowing embers—
Or is it the shadow of shame that falls o'er him?
Ah, No! 'tis the spectre of vengeance, before him.

It was a trying ordeal for all concerned, but full and undeniable identification was absolutely necessary before further proceedings could be made in this important case.

After their first surprise, the ladies, true to their sex, realized the necessity for self control and made ready for their disagreeable errand with all possible speed. They entered a private room at Police Headquarters and, one by one, were ushered into the presence of the prisoner and put through the category of questions necessary to his identification, after which, they were allowed to sit and await the routine of examination until the last informer's signature was affixed to the information given.

Sir Frederic was the first, and as his stern glance rested upon the strangely attenuated form of the wretched young man, he felt that degree of sympathy which borders on contempt for one so weak—so dwarfed in soul and withal so miserable in his weakness,—and briefly stating what he knew of the prisoner and his crimes, he stepped aside and waited anxiously for the entrance of Mrs. Sinclair and Stella. When the former entered the room the man who had called himself her son, rose suddenly from his seat, drawing his still boyish form to its full height, while his fearless eyes looked boldly into hers as if trying hard to force into her mind the thoughts that were evidently at that moment surging through his own.

Slowly a look of bewilderment, perplexity and seeming recognition crept into her face as she gazed, and seeing Sir Frederic standing near, she turned appealingly to him as if requesting aid in the solving of this difficult mystery.

But Sir Frederic's expression only bewildered her more, for it was one of painful consternation.

It was only when the first question was asked regarding her knowledge of the man before her, that she regained composure, and not until some time later did she mention the extraordinary resemblance which she again detected between the prisoner and the husband she still so loved and mourned.

During the entire period of Stella's presence in the room, the accused man leaned jauntily back in his chair and bravely assumed an air of indifferent composure, while his eyes roved admiringly over her innocent face, and much of the old time passion flushed his cheek as he noted with greedy eye the grace and beauty of her finely developed figure.

While his senses vibrated with the magnetic thrill of her presence, the lustre returned to his wide, gray eyes and a smile of pleasure curved his flexible lips, and not even the words of condemnation in her quiet statement were sufficient to counteract the enjoyment which the simple witnessing of her beauty brought him. He had thought her dead on that memorable night when he stood by the ashes of Julia Webber's ruined home, but her marriage to Sir Frederic brought her name so prominently before the public that the error of his supposition was promptly corrected and the few twinges of remorse which he had felt at that time were contemptuously laughed to scorn. Now he was living over again the few brief hours in which she had rested beneath his absolute control, and in the memory of that circumstance, the present was forgotten.

His eyes followed her as she hastened to her husband's side after affixing her signature to the imposing paper, but a moment later a gentle rustle at the door aroused him, and turning suddenly, he found himself face to face with the woman he had stabbed and left for dead, in the gloomy passage of Whitechapel so many months ago. Thoroughly surprised and with genuine alarm now stamped on every feature, he looked wildly about as if to fly, while his cheeks and lips grew white at this unlooked for apparition.

He had supposed Elizabeth dead, and thus far no knowledge of his being suspected of the murder had ever reached him, for he reasoned that the crimes committed in that wretched quarter of London were so numerous and so almost untraceable, that he, like many other red handed assassins, had escaped through a fortunate choice in the location of the deed. So great was the sudden revulsion of thought and theory, that his reason wavered for an instant as he gazed upon the delicate, black robed figure.

The words of Julia Webber's warning were ringing in his ears, and before he could fairly comprehend the terrible situation, the white faced woman extended her arms and with a piercing cry of "Lawrie! Lawrie! my darling, my husband!" threw herself upon his breast, and then for want of a supporting arm, sank helplessly upon the floor at her destroyer's feet.

CHAPTER XXXIII.
"I HAVE NO NAME."

What possession more awful that mortal can name
Than the stigma of passion—the birthright of shame—
The cloud of abasement grows deep and more dense
Till the soul is deformed in its darkness, intense.

It was only for a moment that Elizabeth crouched thus on the floor, for before Sir Frederic could reach her side she had staggered to her feet and confronting the trembling man with eyes grown suddenly haggard like his own, she exclaimed brokenly:—

"Oh, Lawrie! Lawrie! You won my love when my heart was innocent of sin; you deceived me and denied our marriage; you left your child to be born in dishonor and your lawful wife without protection,—but I will gladly forgive it all if you will only right the wrong that you have done our little one by giving her, even at this late hour, her rightful name!"

Throughout her tearful, passionate appeal, the man she called her husband shrank back with lowered lids and hands upraised before his face as if to avert the torrent of reproaches that fell from her long silent lips; but now as she forgot her wrongs and only begged the rightful heritage of her child, the blood rushed violently to his face and rising, he bent unsteadily toward her as with blazing eyes and husky tones he exclaimed excitedly:—

"Name? My God! How can I give that which I never had?"

Then turning almost savagely to the wondering witnesses, he said bitterly, "Coward and cur I may be, but that is my only legacy,—my only inheritance from the parents who brought me into a world of sin and left me, nameless and alone,—an outcast upon society and a leper among those who boast their proud morality."

Then as his gaze rested once more upon his grief stricken wife, he lowered his tones to almost gentleness as he added: "I saved your honor by a legal marriage, but shame for the one honorable act of my life made me deny it:—

"I tried to kill you," he continued recklessly, but Elizabeth, realizing the awful consequences of the dreadful admission, sprang forward, crying sharply, "No! No! Lawrie,—not that! Do not say that!" but he thrust her wildly aside and went on as if no interruption had occurred:

"That was the second honorable impulse of my life. I knew the misery and shame of your surroundings was worse than death and as I had no name to offer you I tried to end your wretchedness" —

Before he could say more the hand of the law was upon him, and a stern but kindly intentioned voice, said briefly, "Hush, man,—you are closing the door of a prison cell upon yourself by your talking; come, answer me and be brief,—are you or are you not Maurice Sinclair?"

"I am not," was the husky answer.

"Are you or are you not, Lawrence Maynard?"

At this question Elizabeth leaned heavily forward on Mrs. Sinclair's arm, straining every nerve in her eagerness to catch his answer.

"I am not," was again the faint reply.

Then the officer turned to the excited group before him and with an attempt to shorten the trying scene, said curtly, "Do any of you know this man, and if so, by what name do you know him?"

There was a moment's silence, then a stranger stepped forward from behind the others and almost simultaneously the two men looked into each other's eyes and exclaimed:

"Dr. Seward!"

"Jack Fenton!"

Then the younger of the two, forgetful of his weaker frame, sprang angrily forward and grasping the physician's shoulder, hissed fiercely between his teeth, "You called me Jack Fenton, but you know that name is false. You, and you only, can tell my father's name; speak, man, and clear the mystery of my birth, or by the God above—"

But the effort was too much for his feeble strength and he sank helplessly to the floor. Worn out by months and years of intense excitement and threatened danger; dependent upon the uncertain issues of chance and speculation for his maintenance and haunted by a morbid thirst for the avenging of that shame and secrecy that dwelt upon his birth, it was little wonder that the shock of present circumstances benumbed his senses.

When at last the room was cleared, Dr. Seward bent above the prostrate man and deep in his own heart the pain of a life's remorse sprang up and nearly overcame him.

How much the young man knew of his part in the awful tragedy, he did not know, but deep in his own heart he felt that the responsibility of this wretched mortal's sins and miseries rested in great measure upon his shrinking shoulders, and satisfied now, beyond a doubt, that this was the child whose parentage he had so long concealed, he turned over and over in his mind the possibilities of yet undoing the wrong which he assisted, so materially, to do, thereby removing from his own accusing conscience the secret that so long had been its burden. But for Mrs. Sinclair's sake the words must yet remain unspoken. The prisoner would be speedily returned to London, and upon Lady Van Tyne he depended for aid in securing for her son, not only all that could possibly be done to make his trial speedy and his condemnation light, but the deathless silence which should save one noble woman from the knowledge of a loved one's treachery. Would Lady Van Tyne do this? Dr. Seward hardly knew, but he trusted that a mother's love would brave the scorn of public censure, and that human sympathy for a suffering sister would raise a shield of silence for the trusting wife's defence.

The Lady Van Tyne was vain and worldly, still it was his only hope, and win or fail, it was for him to put it to the test.

To Sir Frederic, only, he told his plans, then acting upon their mutual decision, he returned at once to England, leaving the unhappy young man safe in the custody of American law and justice.

CHAPTER XXXIV.
THE LADY VAN TYNE WILL FIGHT FOR HER HONOR.

A woman's mercy is a bark
Set forth on life's broad sea to ride,—
Its course ordained, yet veered about
By every shifting wind and tide.

The Lady Van Tyne was standing before the long pier-glass arranging the final touches of her elaborate coiffure when Dr. Seward was announced. The excitement caused by his sudden departure for America had hardly subsided when it was again aroused by his unexpected return.

Even Lady Van Tyne, revolving as she was in the whirlpool of social duties and pleasures, stopped long enough to express some wonder at the eccentricities of her staid and venerable physician. But her eagerness to greet him now as he entered her private sanctum did not deter her from once more altering the position of a jeweled pin in her abundant hair and turning again, glass in hand, to note the effect of her artistic alteration.

"Ah, doctor," she exclaimed, as she laid the costly glass carefully upon the dressing-case, "I heard that you had returned but I hardly expected you would so soon honor me with a call;—but what is the matter? you look ill" she said as she noted the unusual pallor of his face.

"No not ill," was his reply, as he stood looking down upon her while his hands toyed nervously with a heavy walking stick. Then making a determined effort as if to have it over as soon as possible, he said abruptly, "Lady Van Tyne, forgive me, but for nearly thirty years I have kept silence upon this subject, but to-day I must speak. I have found your son, and if ever man needed a mother's love, he does. I beg you to hear his story and then let us try together to undo the sin committed so many years ago." The physician's face was flushed with shame and eagerness when he had finished speaking, but the wave of violent anger that swept across his hearer's features left her with blazing eyes and tightly compressed lips, and for a moment he wondered vaguely what the outcome of her emotions was to be.

It was only an instant's wonderment, for with swift and decided movement she withdrew the heavy portieres, and motioned him to enter a more secluded room, then following, she came close beside him and clutching his arm, exclaimed fiercely, "How dare you speak of this to me? were you not paid for silence as well as for assistance in the matter?"

The physician winced beneath her words but she continued angrily, "learn what you will of this child, but remember, please, that I will hear no word regarding him or his whereabouts. You undertook his concealment,—see you to it that it is continued, at least, so far as I am concerned," and she drew herself to her stateliest carriage before the shrinking form of the unhappy man.

"But he is your first born, dear Lady Van Tyne,—have you no love in your heart for the child of your happy days? No feeling of remorse for the crime committed against humanity? no pity for the unfortunate boy, thrust nameless and alone upon the careless mercy of this cruel, heartless world?"

"You plead well, Dr. Seward," she sneered as the physician wiped the beads of sweat from his heated brow. "You plead for the very child whose abandonment you first suggested, have you forgotten that?"

"Alas, no," said Dr. Seward, sadly. "I have forgotten nothing. I humbly admit the sin which youth and thoughtlessness permitted, but believe me, I have suffered greatly for that error and now when I have found the innocent babe, grown to full manhood, with his nature cramped and dwarfed by bitterness of spirit; his hand turned fiercely against himself and every man's hand against him, I feel that it is our duty, yours and mine, to come forth boldly in his cause and help if possible to redeem from death and eternal condemnation, the human soul we have so inexpressibly wronged.

"It can not be that you, his mother, will refuse to aid me in this undertaking?" he questioned pleadingly.

But the Lady Van Tyne was weary of the subject. The self control that at first deserted her had now returned, and curving her lips in a disdainful smile, she said distinctly, "Dr Seward, I have valued your advice for many years but it seems to me that now your judgment is deserting you. If this is true that you have found the child, I can only say, do what you please regarding the matter, but depend upon it, I shall deny your accusations and defend my position before the world with the unlimited means that you well know are at my disposal. I have the dignity of my family to sustain and the claims of unwelcome offspring shall never interfere between Lady Van Tyne and her social position, so"—she continued, as she drew aside the heavy curtains, "if you are determined to play the fool we may as well shake hands and consider our acquaintance at an end forever."

But Dr. Seward did not touch the jeweled fingers that were extended to him so graciously. He merely bowed his head and passed silently out of her presence, feeling in all humility that the sorrow of the moment was but another expiation of the never forgotten error of his youthful days.

After he had gone the Lady Van Tyne returned again to her mirror and took a long survey of herself in the polished glass, but some way the reflection of her person was not as pleasing as it had been an hour before and she jerked the lace awkwardly about her throat, while wrinkles hitherto unnoticed crept stealthily about her eyes and the wave of fine grey hair upon her brow looked singularly old and unbecoming. She had not deceived herself by her apparent calmness of demeanor during the physician's strange entreaty, and now that she was alone her courage forsook her entirely and she sank heavily upon the sofa in a paroxysm of fear and trembling while she felt the foundations of her respectability shaking beneath her feet and pictured her humiliating position if the truth should ever be revealed. Not a thought of her son's surroundings entered her mind, and, as she finally controlled herself for the evening's pleasure, a prayer for her own protection was the one vague sentiment of her selfish, worldly heart.

It was late that night before Dr. Seward retired to his private office for an hour with his books and drugs, for he had extended his ride after leaving Lady Van Tyne's residence and called upon his friend at the hospital across the bridge. Here his scientific curiosity returned and he again became possessor of the little vial of brownish powder. That night in the privacy of his professional den, he again investigated the mysterious contents.

Over and over again the breakfast bell was rung in the early morning, but not until the household was thoroughly alarmed at his continued absence, did any one think to try the handle of the office door. There they found him, cold and breathless upon the well worn sofa, while by his side upon the carpet was a curious shaped vial, empty, and bearing on one side a label whereupon was written in Dr. Seward's own handwriting, the extraordinary warning, "Death to the Inquisitive."

CHAPTER XXXV.
STELLA AND ELIZABETH.

How pure the passion of a woman's love—
How innocent the heart that bleeds;
The wretch is worshiped like the saints above
In spite of weaknesses and guilty deeds.

The news of Dr. Seward's mysterious death fell like a thunder bolt upon the household he had left so recently across the water.

Mrs. Sinclair mourned sincerely for the loss of a life long friend, and Stella, for a fatherly counsellor.

For hours after the arrival of the cablegram announcing the physician's death, Sir Frederic paced the floor of his apartments, pondering deeply on a secret which he felt must be shared by none. He was thinking of Dr. Seward's suspicions as to the parentage of the young man now safely guarded within the ponderous walls of the "Tombs." It had been only a suspicion and now the one human being who knew aught of the matter was silent in the sleep of death.

It was left for him to speak the words which should wound Mrs. Sinclair's faithful heart and destroy forever the sacred memory which was a part of her very being.

It was plain to him that the unhappy prisoner knew nothing of his birth and only suspected Dr. Seward of knowledge on the subject through some recollection of old associations. If this was the case there could be no harm in remaining altogether silent on the subject, but then, when this conclusion was reached, he thought of Lady Van Tyne and her probable knowledge and realized how impossible it would be to conceal the identity of her son from his mother when the question of his parentage was raised, as it must be, during his trial by English law.

Whether Dr. Seward had succeeded in obtaining an interview with Lady Van Tyne before his death, Sir Frederic did not know, and although greatly distressed, he determined to defer the matter as long as possible as Mrs. Sinclair and Stella were happier now than they had been for many days, not only in their freedom from all supposed relationship to the guilty man, but in the anticipation of a new joy that had recently crept mysteriously within their hearts.

Elizabeth's sorrow was pitiful to behold, but the winds of grief were tempered with kindness, in the fact of her lawful wifehood and the love of her baby girl she found much happiness and comfort.

It was a pleasure to them all one chilly evening as they gathered about the roaring fire, the butler entered and unceremoniously ushered into their presence the jolly old Commander whose story of Maurice Sinclair's death brought them sorrow and rejoicing, and the kindly young officer of the Cunarder whose interest had been the means of so much prosperity to Elizabeth and her child.

"Ha, Ha," laughed the bronzed old Captain as he tossed little Elsa high in the air; "You don't look much as you did on the Steamer, little one. I guess you've anchored in a pleasant port, Ay?"

"Indeed we have sir," responded Elizabeth, softly, as she gave her hand to him in greeting.

"Well, well," he continued, looking appreciatively at her rounded cheeks. "'Pon my soul, I never expected to see you looking like this. Here, Mate, look at her red cheeks," he continued gaily, turning to the young officer.

The young man blushed like a girl, for all his manly proportions, as he took Elizabeth's timid hand and bent his head modestly as she said, "I have *you* to thank for my home and happiness, Mr. Moore. You were the first to think of me when I was lying sick in that dreadful place."

"Indeed, Madam," he answered hurriedly, "it was the Chinaman that mentioned the matter to me, you must not forget him."

"That is so, what became of the Ching Chong, Sir Frederic?" asked the Captain as he lowered himself slowly into the massive rocker by Mrs. Sinclair's side.

Sir Frederic told him briefly of his last interview with Sam Lee and the capture of the imposter, touching as lightly as possible on the facts of the case in deference to Elizabeth's presence, and both men sat silently and listened with great interest to the recital.

When it was ended the Captain asked anxiously, "Did he give his name or any clue to his identity?"

"He said that Jack Fenton was not his name, although he had been called by that, and only knew himself as an illegitimate child, cast off by his parents and reared by those who were equally ignorant of his birth with himself.

"There is no doubt in my mind, Captain, but that he is the other lad in your story, but you shall see him yourself to-morrow and that will remove the last suspicion of doubt regarding his identity."

"And this Chinaman," continued the Captain, "you say he conversed with him in that heathenish tongue, that in spite of a dozen stops in Chinese ports, I could never make head or tail out of, does he give him a name or know anything of his past?"

Here, Elizabeth rose quietly and making some trivial excuse, passed hastily from the room, but not so quickly but that Stella, who had both felt and seen her uneasiness, immediately joined her outside the door.

"Oh, Lady Atherton," Elizabeth cried as Stella drew her closely to her side in mute sympathy when they were alone. "How dreadful it all is. To think that the man I loved and trusted; the father of my darling child, should be nameless, friendless and alone, with sin upon his soul and no one to breathe a word of sympathy in his hour of need. Oh, Lawrie!" she sobbed, "If I could only come to you."

"But, dear Lizzie," whispered Stella, "You must think of yourself and Elsa first of all. You have suffered enough and it can do no possible good for you to go to him. Wait, Lizzie, wait until he is penitent and expresses a wish for his wife's forgiveness."

"Yes, I know that he does not care," cried Elizabeth, "but my heart aches for him and I would gladly forgive all if he would only say that he loved me. Oh, My Husband. You were merciful,—you spared my honor and gave my child a stainless birth when, body and soul, I would have been your slave. Yes, I too, will be merciful," she continued suddenly with a determined voice as she raised her streaming eyes to Stella's face.

"Let me go to him, dear Lady Atherton, my place is at my husband's side. Let me plead for him at his trial and bear with him the penalty of his sins."

"Do you love him so dearly, Lizzie?" asked Stella sadly.

"I loved him once—Yes, yes I love him now," she added,—then facing Stella she asked abruptly, "would you not do the same? Would you not cling to him and work for him, if the man you loved was trembling on the verge of awful danger?"

"I don't know," said Stella, doubtfully. Then a proud smile curved her lips and her dark eyes flashed as she added, slowly, "I am afraid, dear, that my love would never stand the test of sin and crime in one I loved. Weakness and error I would shield; I would face danger and bear humiliation, but I feel that I could never endure to blush with shame for a loved one's infamy or drink the dregs of degradation, although pressed to my lips by my husband, himself. No! Lizzie," she said decidedly, "when my lover falls from his pedestal of honor and virtue and descends to the crimes and vices of this earth, I shall cease to love him, and though it tore the weak, fleshy heart from my bosom, I would never voluntarily look upon his face again." There was silence for several moments between the two when she finished speaking, but at last Stella rose and said gently, "Wait here a little and compose yourself, dear, while I return to our friends and when you join us again there shall be nothing said to distress you, for I know," she added roguishly, "the young officer has not come to see either mamma or me and you know Elsa is hardly old enough to receive young gentlemen callers without her mother to act as chaperone."

When Stella returned to the parlor it was as she thought. Her husband had made his guests familiar with Elizabeth's story and she was a little surprised to see the young officer holding Elsa carefully on his knee while his eyes blazed and his features were set in a look of stern resolve that boded no good for the villain of the narrative, should he by any chance cross his path.

CHAPTER XXXVI.
A LAST ESCAPE.

Death frees his body, but his soul

Goes on to its predestined state:—

But who are we that we should judge—

Or name an erring brother's fate;

The wheels of the law moved slowly but steadily forward until but one short day remained before the extradition of the nameless prisoner to the legal guardianship of his native country. Much interest had been excited in his case and great scope given the imagination of the curious regarding his identity, but all to no avail. The cloud upon his birth pursued him and now that Dr. Seward was dead there seemed little fear of its ever being lifted.

None but the idly inquisitive seekers after morbid sensations called upon him in his prison home until the day before his anticipated departure, when a Mongolian, wearing the full regalia of his country, begged a brief audience with the carefully guarded man.

No one knew what was said during that short interview as the conversation baffled the linguistic ability of the Irish guard, but when it was over he was promptly ushered out by the son of Erin who had listened with open mouthed astonishment to their unintelligible chatterings.

It was only a brief five minutes that the guard remained away, but when he returned to his post, after seeing the Celestial visitor safely outside the building, he thought he detected an unusual odor, and going immediately to his prisoner's door demanded to know "what koind of shmell the grasy yaller shkin had lift behoind him, to be shure!"

But there was no answer to his inquiry and promptly opening the door he was horrified to find that in spite of all his vigilance his prisoner had escaped him. Not by disappearance of body, for the still cold form remained, but by flight of soul, instantaneous and complete, while the sickish odor of some unknown drug spoke only too plainly of the method employed for his escape from earthly bondage.

For a moment the horrified guard was speechless with concern, then closing the door silently, he repaired to the warden's office, and in a few short hours all New York was ringing with the news of the mysterious death and clamoring wildly for the capture of the prisoner's only visitor.

CHAPTER XXXVII.
FIVE YEARS AFTER.

And after all perhaps 'tis best
To make no mention of the past;
The clouds have vanished and to all
The peaceful days have come at last.

Five years have passed away since that death in the lonely prison cell, but from that day, Sam Lee disappeared as completely from the gaze of man as if he, too, had journeyed to the world from whence there is no returning.

Search was unavailing and inquiry and investigation alike, fruitless.

The autopsy made upon the dead man's body revealed nothing other than asphyxiation by an unknown drug, but whether administered by his own or other hands, was never ascertained.

Men reasoned, argued and theorized, and at last lost interest.

For Elizabeth's sake, Sir Frederic saw that the body was decently interred and then made haste to return once more to Portland Place, as it was Stella's ardent wish that her child should be born in the home so dear to her own youthful associations.

Little Archie is now nearly five years old and baby Millie just turned one, but they have thus early demonstrated their importance in the Atherton family, and no one dreams for a moment of denying their claims to attention and worship.

Mrs. Sinclair is radiantly happy.

Little Archie is her husband's namesake, and on him she lavishes so much of her tender love that Stella often wonders if baby Millie will not some day look with jealous eyes upon her grandma's preference.

The children are frequent visitors at the house in G—St., where Elsa watches carefully over their frolics with the conscious dignity of her mature years.

Elizabeth thought at first that she could not endure to live again beneath the walls that had been the scenes of her perilous infatuation, but of late a peaceful smile lights up her lovely features and the old house has been turned completely upside down with her tasteful renovations.

Perhaps little Elsa explains matters somewhat when she grasps Mr. Morris' extended hand and leading him gaily to her playmates, says confidentially, "This is my new papa, Archie, mamma says so!" and "Mamma," who has entered at that moment, comes blushingly forward to be held for a moment in her young husband's arms, while the first deep feeling of perfect love thrills her long sorrowing heart with joy unspeakable.

As for Sir Frederic, he has watched carefully for any signs of knowledge on the part of Lady Van Tyne regarding the suspicions which Dr. Seward so conscientiously revealed to him, but the years go by and there is no word.

The Lady Van Tyne sits calmly on her pedestal of virtue, and although its foundations are of gold, still there is enough of that precious metal to secure her position for many years to come, and positive that no word of hers will ever destroy her social prominence, Sir Frederic locks the guilty secret in his heart and turning to the sweet faced women whom he loves, breathes silently a solemn vow of "Death to the Inquisitive."